A LAND OF MEN AND
GIANTS

TONY DORAN
AN AUTOBIOGRAPHY

A LAND OF MEN AND
GIANTS

TONY DORAN
AN AUTOBIOGRAPHY

HERO BOOKS

HERO BOOKS

PUBLISHED BY HERO BOOKS
1 WOODVILLE GREEN
LUCAN
CO. DUBLIN
IRELAND
www.herobooks.ie
Hero Books is an imprint of Umbrella Publishing

First Published 2017

A CIP record for this book is available from the British Library

ISBN 9781910827031

Printed in Ireland with Print Procedure Ltd
Cover design and typesetting: Jessica Maile
Cover photograph: Sportsfile

Contents

Dedication

To Mary,
Our children Therese, Noelle, Tony, Pat and Marie,
Our grandchildren Aoife and Liam,
And daughter and son in-laws Kelly and Gavin

Acknowledgments

Thanks to my late parents, Willie and Francie, and to my brothers, Bill, Joe, Colm and the late Sean, for all of their help and encouragement over a long number of years.

My wife, Mary has been such a major player in everything I achieved since our marriage in 1977. We had very little time for a honeymoon once we married on a Saturday as I had to be back for training with Buffers Alley the following midweek (for a county semi-final on the Sunday) – in fact, I think most of those days we were away we were out pucking a ball about!

Mary's involvement in athletics and camogie made her well aware of the sacrifices that were so often needed. Likewise, when our family was small, not alone was the workload in the house left down to her, but she also had to keep tabs on what was happening on the farm while I was training or off at matches.

I thank Mary for everything, and I thank our children, Therese, Noelle, Tony, Pat and Marie, for all of their help with odd jobs that always needed to be done. Marie, I suppose, escaped most of that as when I played my last match she was only two weeks old! But I am glad that they have all shared the passion of their parents and that they themselves have achieved success at schools, colleges, club and county level.

While Mary and I are indebted to my family, we are equally thankful for the love and support of the Hobbs family, Teresa especially. Mary's father, and brothers and sisters, also were ever present in their support for us, as were my other sisters-in-law, Bridie, Betty and Anne.

Mary and I needed the help of many babysitters down through the years of my career, and no matter how often they were called upon they were never found wanting when help was needed. Lynn and Patty Lacey dug us out of many a hole, and they told us it was never a problem for them – even when the 'whole gang' were left off in their home!

Before my own children were born, help was also needed in the Doran household after our mother passed away. There were five men in that household, and even though our neighbour Mary Martin had 17 children in her own home, she was there for me and my brothers on an almost daily basis, cooking and cleaning and washing for us. For that care and support, we are forever grateful.

To all of my neighbours and friends in the Alley and the surrounding area who were always so willing to lend a hand with farmwork and the milk round, a sincere and everlasting thank you. Likewise, when I had no transport to training in Enniscorthy or wherever, there was always someone to offer a lift or give me a loan of a car.

I am equally thankful to all of the suppliers on the milk round, hauliers and farmers, for bringing in their own milk, and all of the Ballycanew Creamery staff for their support and assistance to me at all times.

To all of my fellow players and mentors from the Monageer Boolavogue Rackard League team, where it all started in 1956; Gorey CBS during my time there; Realt na Mara juvenile (under-16) team with whom I played my first ever game of football in 1959; and the Ferns minors in 1961 and '62. Thanks to you all for giving me the chance to be part of your teams.

To Buffers Alley from 1959 to 1993, and Wexford from 1963 to 1984, it was always a great honour to pull on the green and gold, and the purple and gold, and to share the same playing field with so many outstanding men. To every person I played with or against, and at whatever level, club or county, it was always an honour to compete. Neither can I ever forget the Wexford Masters (over-40s) hurlers who won the All-Ireland title in 1991, and our mentors, for their dedication and great will to win which was really unbelievable. This was a group that included some men who had reached the very top of the game already in their careers, and others who perhaps had spent most of their lives at junior club level, but we all came together and gelled as a unit which was a great credit to everyone concerned. This victory also gave me the honour of captaining, for the very first time, a Wexford team that claimed a national title.

To all team mentors at club and county level, and also to club and county board officers who served during my time as a player, I am greatly indebted to each and every one of you. Neither can I ever forget the supporters of my club and county who were always an inspiration. While we shared a lot of disappointing days, we also had many joyous occasions which will live long in the memory.

While my hurling career is dealt with thoroughly in this book, I also found the time to play a bit of football – and I wish to acknowledge the heart and passion of all the Buffers Alley footballers that was demonstrated every time we took to the field. For years we did not even have a football, but eventually we enjoyed some success too and we were determined enough to win county titles at intermediate, junior and junior B grades. From 1967 to '72 I was fortunate enough to represent Wexford footballers at junior level, and to enjoy our journey to a Leinster final in 1972 even though we lost to Offaly. Late in 1972 I made my only appearance as a Wexford senior footballer when I travelled as an extra with a very understrength team to play Limerick in the Gaelic Grounds. I was introduced as a sub in the second-half and ended up playing on Eamonn Cregan, who was quite a useful footballer, whereas I had just a 'left leg' and was of limited ability – but to everyone I played with as a county footballer for those few years, a very sincere thank you.

To each and every person I 'hit up' against – players and supporters, for and against – I am honoured to have known you! It was a journey that included sad and disappointing days, and so many joyful occasions. But it was everything to me.

Thanks everyone for the memories!

To all of my socialising friends, all of the way back to the 'two-bob' card drives and socials in Monamolin, Monageer and Boolavogue; to the top showband venues like the Tara Ballroom in Courtown, the Talbot in Wexford, the KMH Kilmuckridge, the Castle in Enniscorthy, Adamstown, and the numerous marquees of that 1960s and 70s era, thanks for the good times.

To all of the Alley clubhouse card players and our regular Sunday night patrons, thanks for your friendship and company. Many have sadly passed away, but thankfully there is still a hard core continuing a brilliant tradition that is now going back almost 40 years.

Finally, to Liam Spratt, a special thank you for sitting down with me to begin with and giving of your time to encourage me to tell my story. And to Liam and Anne Hayes, and the team at Hero Books, for bringing this book to life.

Tony Doran,
October, 2017

PROLOGUE

My father's family was a longtail family.

He was one of three families. His father was a widower when he got married... his mother was a widow. His mother had five daughters... his father had two daughters.

My father had seven half-sisters, and there were just two boys in the third family. His brother died at a very early age. They used to have a small shop... and the little boy got smothered in a chest of flour that you would have had in shops at that time. It was an awful tragedy. It was something that I never heard my father talk about, to be honest.

All three families were named Doran... his mother's first husband was a Doran also. All the members of the three families were called Doran, and the girls from both families were all around the same ages.

My mother, Frances Walsh from Tomnaboley, Boolavogue, came from a family of four surviving children, three girls and a boy.

There were two other children in the family who died as infants, or very young in childhood.

My father farmed. He had roughly 100 acres altogether, and in that time it was a little bit of everything. Dairying wasn't a big thing in the area when I was a small boy. That would only have started when I was growing up.

He was a big GAA man... a Buffers Alley man all his life, and he would always bring us around to all of the games. At the time when he was playing with the club they would have won a county junior championship in 1928... they lost an intermediate final by one point in '31. He got as far as playing junior for Wexford... but he always played a big part in the club. He was chairman for a number of years and he was always in the background helping out all of his life. He never missed a game.

WILLIE DORAN died in the early afternoon of November 29, 1970. He died in Wexford Park as four of his sons, 33 year-old Bill, 26 year-old Joe, 24 year-old Tony, and Colm, just 21, the baby of the family of five boys in total played for Buffers Alley in the county senior hurling final. Willie Doran was 63 years old. A massive heart attack claimed him almost instantaneously.

The game was never stopped.

The Alley in their green jerseys with yellow sashes had the run on the green and white coloured Shamrocks – from the foot of Vinegar Hill – from early on in the game. Buffers Alley would claim their second Wexford senior title by a commanding 21 points, 4-16 to 1-4, which was a whole different ball game to their first title two years earlier when they had a single point to spare over the purple and gold of Faythe Harriers, 5-6 to 4-8.

Bill was centre-back.

Colm on his left.

Joe in the middle of the field.

Tony in at full-forward.

We were told at half-time that he was after having a turn. He was obviously dead by then... but we weren't told that.

I actually saw a person being taken away on a stretcher past the back of the town goal during the first-half. And then for some reason I turned around a second time, and I saw Pat Nolan, who was the Wexford goalie at that time... I saw Pat by the stretcher and it struck me that it was my father who was on the stretcher.

Pat was a cousin of ours and a close friend of my father. He realised that I had seen something, but he waved me away, and told me it was okay, to play ahead.

You'd wonder why I turned around the first time, and... for no reason, why I turned back around the second time?

I don't know.

He was brought to the hospital. The four of us were kept apart in the dressing room and I don't remember talking to my brothers. The club officials had talked amongst themselves at half-time about calling off the match, but they decided that the best thing was to go ahead... finish the game.

The Shamrocks had won the championship in '69... they beat us in the semi-final. We had won in '68, and the 1970 final was the decisive clash between the two teams. I'd say it was one of the best county finals I ever played in. We were able to concentrate on the game alright... but near the end we were so well ahead, and the interest in the game was gone. That was hard. The fizz was out of the game... it was done and dusted. I found myself looking over at the officials on the sideline and I saw a neighbour of ours, Peter O'Brien, who was a teammate in my father's playing days... and I could see him looking upset... throwing his arms in the air. He was talking to my mother's brother, John Walsh who had gone to the hospital with my father. John had come back into the ground.

I knew that was it at that stage.

I knew my father was gone.

In the dressing room we were told that he had died. There was no presentation of the cup or anything like that... it was just handed over to Pierie Butler, our captain... the cup was just handed *to him. There was no big deal made of it.*

The four of us got dressed and headed to the hospital. My father was there... still in his street clothes... lying there in the mortuary. My mother wasn't there... she very seldom went to matches. There were a good few people around him... he was lying there on a cold slab.

A neighbour went home from the game... Fr Tom Doyle... he broke the news to her. When she saw him coming in the door she knew there was something wrong... she probably thought that one of us had got a serious injury in the game. She never got over it. She died just over 13 months later... heart problems... she had been diagnosed a day or two before she died with a blockage in an artery, and she was being sent to hospital in Dublin. She died the night before she was due to travel.

Frances Walsh, who would become Frances Doran, died in her bed in the family home which, according to local folklore, had one gable wall planted in the parish of Monamolin and the other gable wall holding up in the parish of Boolavogue. Frances Doran was 61 years of age.

Her five boys were all living at home at the time of her passing. Joe was working as a sales rep for Townsend Flahavan of Kilmacthomas in Waterford. The other four were working the Doran land.

Sean, the second eldest boy, was the non-hurling member of the family, though he would take his place in the goals when the others, and some neighbours, would have a bit of a game at home. Sean never played in a club game for Buffers Alley. He passed away at the age of 60 in 1999.

The boys liked the land, and on the Doran land also, across the road from the family home was one of the Doran fields that doubled as a Buffers Alley GAA pitch until 1971. The Doran boys would kick a ball around there, but the more serious business in the field was done with stick and sliotar. All the boys had to do was cross that narrow country road. It was a temptation every hour of the day, but Willie Doran would see to it that work, which he had parceled out amongst them, would always be done.

Until his boys got older, of course, when Willie would agree with them that a game of hurling was first priority.

Willie and Frances' three youngest sons headed off to the Christian Brothers in Gorey when they had finished up in the local national school, but, for Tony, rattling along the full 11 miles by bicycle into the local town was not something that held his interest for very long.

In the winter... or bad days, our father would drive us in his car. Now and again that might happen, but other than that it was bicycles... bad bicycles.

I didn't stay there too long either now. It was always a question of how quickly you could get out of it. I didn't stay for the intermediate certificate, and when I heard one of my brothers saying he was finishing up in the CBS I thought I should leave as well. I wouldn't say my parents were happy about it... but it happened anyhow. I don't remember any questions being asked by the school. Most lads of my age were doing the same thing, and going home to work on the farm full time.

Most of the work on the farm was fairly labour intensive at that time and there was always enough for us all to do.

Cows were milked by hand.... at that stage a good few, maybe 20, give or take, had to be milked twice a day... we didn't see a first milking machine till I was 20 years of age I'd say... they were a scarce commodity at that time... sure people were nearly afraid of them.

Milking was my chief job.

Tony Doran, when asked, doesn't make a great fist of explaining the origination of the name Buffers Alley. He replies that nobody really knows. One hundred yards from where he was born and raised there is a crossroads, and it is known as Buffers Alley crossroads.

Nobody knows where in history the name came from, but that is what the club is called. Different people have tried to get a take on where the name came from... and they couldn't really get anything on it. One theory is that it was a sort of a buffer zone, where a tribe of people met. And there was an alley there as well, and it became known as Buffers Alley.

Locally there are numerous theories as to the story behind the name. The name may have come from the surname of a general who had served in the Boer War. There is also a claim that it sprouted up as a meeting place for boxers known as Buffers. But Buffers Alley as a club was rooted in local fields a few years before the Gaelic Athletic Association formally unveiled itself to the Irish public in 1884.

There were no jerseys in the beginning, just yellow sashes handed out and worn over work shirts. However, green jerseys with the same yellow sashes were on display when Buffers Alley claimed silverware, in 1905, for the first time in the club's history. That was a junior hurling title, and another one followed 23 years after that. The club remained on a back burner in Wexford for quite some time. There was not another junior title until 1951. They stayed in the senior ranks for three years before about-turning, and heading back to junior hurling. In 1962 it was decided to have a shot at the intermediate championship, and in '65 they won it. Buffers Alley amalgamated with Oulart The Ballagh and also won the under-21 championship the same year; and again in 1966.

There was something stirring, at last, in the club and in 1966 they entered the senior championship once more. They got to the final in '67 and came face-to-face for the first time – and at the same time beginning a long and tantalising battle – with the famous black and amber hoops of Nickey Rackard's great Rathnure. Buffers Alley were well beaten. Eighteen points was the difference between the teams, and there would be many more painful, always sobering experiences for teams from the Alley when the shared the greatest stage in Wexford hurling with the men from the far west of the county.

In 1956 Nickey Rackard started what was called the Rackard League. Two schools in the parish came together to play in that. That was my first time to play a hurling game... got to the semi-final the first year. Rackard refereed one game which was unbelievable... to have him... a God... in the middle of the field with us. It was a quarter-final game when a combination of Monageer and Boolavogue schools defeated Ballyoughter.

First Wexford match I was ever at in Croke Park was the '55 All-Ireland semi-final against Limerick. Joe had been brought to the Leinster final... I was brought to the semi-final. John Walsh, Johnny Fowler and a few others would travel with my father to the matches. It would be packed out in the old car.... usually, you'd be sitting on a knee. There could be at least seven people in the car.

I can't remember what time we left the house, but I remember the plans being made during the week and the first part of the plan was to get eight o'clock mass in Arklow, which was over 20 miles from our home. And near Cabinteeley, on the south side of Dublin, there was a man who had a farm and he would boil the water on the side of the road for us for the tea. We had the sandwiches made the night before.

We wouldn't get to Dublin that quickly.

We'd be travelling fairly slowly.

My father was a Cusack Stand man... and any time I went to Croke Park after that I'd nearly always go to the Cusack... seldom the Hogan Stand. There was terracing on the bottom level, and seating on top. We were sitting up on top. We were there early to get tickets.

The only Wexford hurler I would have ever seen in the flesh up to then was Paddy Kehoe, who was one of the greats in Wexford... football and hurling, usually around the half-forward line. He called into the farm through work sometimes... he worked with a lime company.

All we did was listen to the radio whenever Wexford were playing... and we'd be eating the papers as well.

We beat Limerick and went on to win the All-Ireland that year. I was out of the car by then. The first All-Ireland final I was at was 1960. From '55 on I was going to a good few other matches... we beat Tipp in '60. I was in the car in '56 to see Wexford play

Galway again in the All-Ireland semi-final.

But '60 was my first All-Ireland final.

Rackard?

He was a big man... strong as a bull... and Rackard was the man to drive the team. When we were playing in the field across the road as kids we all pretended we were Nickey Rackard... nobody else. But the three Rackards were all big men.

Nickey stood out for so many reasons... for taking frees... scoring goals, and that was a big thing for us all... he was taking 21-yard frees and he was never going to tap them over the bar... he was going to go for goal every time.

Goals!!!!!

Tony Doran was also a man who would have goals in his bloodstream. And by the finish of his career with Wexford he would be right up there with Rackard himself in the scoring charts. Rackard is No.1 in Wexford scoring history.

The giant of a man from the foot of Mount Leinster hit the back of the net 152 times for his county – in 101 appearances over a 15 years career. Tony Doran, in a 19 years career, and 187 appearances, successfully went for goal 131 times.

Doran had the advantage of a longer career alright but, significantly, Doran never took one free for Wexford down through all those years. Unlike Rackard, he never stood on the 21-yards line with the uppermost thought of rifling the ball through a thicket of defenders on the goal-line.

I always had goals on my mind, I reckon... nearly all the time... maybe too much so. There was so much goalmouth action in our day. The sliotar was different that time too, and didn't go as far. I always looked, first of all, to see if there was a goal on.

Like a lot of fellas, I was goal hungry.

Goalkeepers always seemed to be an awful lot busier than they are today... there was always more action around them. I think the fact the ball was not as good and would not go as far... it made keepers legitimate targets... but they were able to defend themselves too.

They had to defend themselves.

Wexford's only All-Ireland hurling title had been as far back as 1910. The county might as well have claimed the title in Roman times, for all the use or inspiration it was for young lads like Tony Doran. With teams lining out with 17 men, Wexford had accounted for Limerick in the All-Ireland decider that year, slicing them open six times in the first-half alone and retiring at the interval 6-0 to 3-1 in front. Rich Doyle had scored three of those, and would take another after the break, but despite the fact that Wexford came out on top in a 13-goal thriller, the magnificence of Doyle and Co was buried treasure. Wexford had better fortunes with the big ball game, until the age of the Rackards.

In 1954, Tony Doran and pups like him with hurls in their hands, listened into matches and heard their elders talk about Wexford's exploits as they put up an audacious 25-33 in three games against Kilkenny, Dublin and Antrim on their way to the All-Ireland final. Five goals were put past Kilkenny. Rackard helped himself to five more in a 8-5 to 1-4 trouncing of Dublin, and a further 12 goals were up on the scoreboard after Wexford's name at the close of the All-Ireland semi-final. Rackard's personal haul that day was 7-7. But Christy Ring was seeking his eight All-Ireland medal and Cork were not to be stopped in the All-Ireland final.

It was a young Limerick team that Tony Doran got to see on his first big day out in Croke Park in 1955. They had managed to slip through the Tipperary-Cork axis, and with Mick Mackey furnished with a whistle on the training field they had run the legs off Clare in the Munster final. The fear of God was sent hurtling through the bodies of younger Wexford supporters when they read in the national newspapers that it was not Limerick that Wexford were meeting in the All-Ireland semi-final... but 'Mackey's Greyhounds'.

Wexford were two points down at half-time, and to the Doran family and their friends in the upper tier of the Cusack Stand, the old legs of their countymen looked to be a problem. The second-half was a different story. Wexford won 2-12 to 2-3. Limerick scored a single point in that half. *'I expect strength and stamina to prove superior to youth and speed,'* wrote Padraig Puirseal in *The Irish Press* the day before the game. Puirseal hit the nail on the head.

Tony Doran sat at home on All-Ireland final day in 1955 as Galway stood between Wexford and what had seemed the impossible for so many years. Up in Croke Park, the Wexford team was unchanged. Billy Rackard was centre-back, his brother Bobby in the corner. At centre-forward was Ned Wheeler, the Kehoes either side of him. In front of them stood Nickey Rackard and Tim Flood. Wheeler and Rackard grabbed two first-half goals, but Galway were two ahead at the change of ends. Those huddled around the radio in homes all over Wexford heard Rackard and Paddy Kehoe going to work for the decisive score of the whole day, and serving up the opportunity for Tim Flood to whack the ball home. It finished 3-13 to 2-8. And when Wexford retained their All-Ireland title the following year, Tony Doran was again missing from the passenger list for his father's car. A Padge Kehoe goal had Wexford four up against Cork at half-time. With 10 minutes remaining, Ring's heroics helped Cork to squeeze in front by a solitary point for the first and only time on a long and worrying afternoon. But it finished 2-14 to 2-8 to Wexford thanks to a goal and three points from Nickey Rackard, who would retire from the county scene the following year.

But, in 1960, Wexford would win their third All-Ireland hurling title in six scintillating years, and Tony Doran would get to witness his first All-Ireland final.

Wexford, in 1959, had failed to reach the Leinster final for the first time in a decade, finding Dublin a handful. New blood had been introduced in '60, and Wexford were given very little hope against Tipperary in the All-Ireland final. The likes of Tony Wall, John Doyle, Theo English, Donie Nealon and Jimmy Doyle were legends of the game, and Nickey Rackard seemed long retired. In the final, the Wexford selectors named John Nolan, who was a brother of our goalie Pat, and he made his championship debut. He would be looking to keep tabs on the unstoppable Jimmy Doyle, and what chance did the Oylegate man have? Tim Flood came out of retirement to take a place in the corner. Wexford appeared to be a team rolling the dice.

But they led 1-5 to 0-2, thanks to a Padge Kehoe goal from a free, and a goal from 'Hopper' McGrath in the second-half left Tipperary stunned.

Nolan would hold Doyle scoreless from play. Billy Rackard was imperious as he stood in the gateway to the Wexford defence. Up front, Kehoe at 35 years of age, seemed to control the tempo of the entire afternoon, and Wexford's 2-15 to 0-11 victory was perfectly believable long before the finish.

Back home in Wexford, it wasn't a question of where a teenage Tony Doran wanted to play on the field. He always found himself chosen to play up front, and asked to do damage.

I was always half forward and midfield... never in the backs... never remember ever being back there... never, ever recall playing in the backs. I don't know, in the age group I found myself, I was probably a big lump of a fella for my age. Midfield was the closest I ever got to our own goals.

My first real game was in a Rackard league match against Oylegate... came on as a sub at half-time, and I was put in at corner-forward. I remember getting on a ball on the end line near the corner flag, and I was just happy to hit the ball... that was the big thing... I made contact with it.

I hit it and... it went straight over the end line. On the way home from that first competitive hurling game played in Doran's Field in Mountdaniel The Ballagh, I was chiselled out by my father never to do that again. After that, he never said much to me... any time I played, whether I was good or bad. He was someone who never interfered.

Our parishes... our club Buffers Alley... it was seen as something like a Cinderella area by those who picked Wexford teams. I was the first player from the place to get picked for the Wexford seniors. But I played for the minors before that... went to a trial match on the Tuesday before the Leinster minor semi-final, and got my place.

By then, however, Tony Doran was already a regular on the Buffers Alley team, getting his first run when he was 16 years-old in an intermediate championship semi-final. He was selected at left half-forward, and had no fears.

It was fairly tough, but you didn't really think of getting a bang. Good honest to God tough teams, that's all I can remember when I started out with the club. There were lots of tough games... lots of rows, but as long as I was playing I was happy enough.

Ger Dempsey (the father of Wexford star, Tom)... as part of his work he'd be passing our home place one day every week or so. Bill was on the road and Ger stopped and they got talking... the match was the following Sunday and at that time there wasn't as much emphasis on training... they were talking about who was available... and who wasn't available and so forth and... and I remember well Ger looking over at me and saying... 'That fella over there... he's big enough to be playing!'

And I was playing the following Sunday in Ferns.

We played Davidstown/Courtnacuddy... we won by a point, and I scored a point. I got a ball out on the wing and let fly, and it ended up in the right place. I kept my place for the final... we played Hollow Rangers and they beat us by five points in Wexford Park.

When you're 16 years of age you are not worried about anything. There's no such thing as pressure playing in a stadium. Life is just perfect getting the chance to play there.

My older brothers were more established on the team, though at that stage Joe would still have been a minor.

Bill wasn't that big, as a centre-back... 5' 9" or thereabouts, and as centre-backs went at the time he might have been quite small. He wouldn't have been the biggest but he was able to read the game very well and he got away with it for a good many years! In his last year he had moved to full-forward, inside me... he'd moved to the other end of the field as you do when you get older. I was centre-forward. He was strong, stocky. Joe was a lighter figure, with a big swing... we always told him that anyhow!

You'd see the swing coming for long enough... but in the middle of the field he was one of those lads who always kept the ball moving. His biggest strength was that he was one of those lads who always got stuck in and maybe he didn't look the most *stylish, but he would have always been in the thick of it. He may have been light, but he was wiry... and didn't flinch. He was always looking to get the ball into the forwards very quickly.*

Buffers Alley got a right hiding when they won their way back to the intermediate final the following year in 1963, and Davidstown/Courtnacuddy served up the grand total of 11-9, against the Alley's 2-6. Two years later, in '65, Buffers Alley were Wexford intermediate champions when they met Liam Mellows in Gorey, and had too much in hand, winning 3-11 to 1-4.

There was no real indication that Buffers Alley would become a powerhouse in Wexford hurling, and do so in double-quick time. They got to the senior quarter-finals in '66 which was considered a respectable performance, but with a young crew beginning to take up seating space in the senior dressing-room they surprised most observers by winning through to the senior final the next year. They got thumped by Rathnure, 4-13 to 1-4.

Maybe a bit of a surprise... but we were having a turnover of players for a few years before that... young fellas were coming in after winning a couple of under-21 championships, but Rathnure beat us in our first final in '67. The day completely passed us by. We came back in '68 and won our first county title, beating the Harriers in the final.

By this stage a fourth Doran, Colm had come onto the scene, playing at wing forward. When he was growing up we all thought that he was going to be too small and delicate to ever figure on a team, but he soon strengthened up and when he moved to half-back a couple of years later he really blossomed.

We'd had a lot of meetings with the Harriers... we'd played them in a quarter-final in '67 and played a draw... played in the first round in '68... and it was a draw and they beat us by a point in the replay... and a losers group operated that year in the championship and we came back in through that losers group. We beat the Harriers by a point in the final in our fifth meeting in just over a year.

Games were hard and fair between us... but got maybe a little bit firey in the final. I was actually playing on Willie Murphy... we were Wexford team-mates.

Wexford had just won the All-Ireland.

Willie was playing centre-back for the Harriers. There was a little bit of an altercation in the first 15 or 20 minutes and, anyhow... Willie got sent off. It was severe enough of a decision... there were no yellow cards or anything at that stage.

I really don't know what happened? A ball was coming down on us early on and as far as I recall I was spreading my arms to protect myself... and get the ball... and one of my arms connected with Willie's head... he got a nick on it. It was an elbow or a fist holding the stick, I think... it was an accident, but maybe Willie felt that I had done it intentionally... I don't know (Tony laughs to himself in a high pitched tone).

The next ball came and... Willie must have let fly (more laughter)... I wasn't badly injured or anything, but he got the line straight away.

I think we were level at half-time and the Harriers got a bit of a run on us in the second-half. I think they were eight points up... and we hadn't scored in the half... we had gone completely out of the game.

And we had a fella playing wing forward... Bill Murphy, who single-handedly dug us out of a hole by scoring two goals and three points in the last eight minutes (laughs) to win that first title for us.

Yah! (Tony says 'Yah', in a satisfying way a lot as he signs off on his memories of the old games).

I was only average I'd say, that day... only average now... yah! You talk about long seasons and things now, but that final was actually played on the eighth of December... Wexford had won the All-Ireland and there had been a full stop during the whole summer while that was going on... there was a big back log of fixtures.

And we ended up playing every Sunday for a good few weeks

because we had to come through the losers group. That was a big advantage to us because we got five or six matches in a short time.

The first Buffers Alley team to win the Wexford senior hurling championship had three families making up nine of the team.

There were four Dorans.

Three Butlers, and two Murphys.

The Murphys, Joe and Liam, were first cousins of the Dorans (Jack Hall was another cousin of the Dorans). And the Butlers, Pierie, Henry and Mick, may as well have been in the family, such was the tight bond that had been born in the Buffers Alley dressing room.

That's how it was for a few years afterwards. The two Murphys were getting near the end of their days on the team... in their thirties at the time. And my brother Bill and Bill Murphy were also over the 30 mark... even though they won a couple of championships after. The three Dorans that remained and the three Butlers still made up the backbone of the team for a good few years afterwards.

Mick Kinsella, who'd also been on the Wexford team, was a big player. He broke a finger a few weeks before the county final and he was moved out to the wing from centre-back. Paddy Sinnott was captain of the team that year but missed out on the final because of an illness which struck him about 10 days before it. He wasn't even at the game. He was at home in his sick-bed, and we all went to him in his home with the cup afterwards.

Younger lads were coming in... Paddy Kavanagh, 23 at that time... played a fair bit with Wexford afterwards... he was playing full-back and Larry Harney was 19, and Ternie Murphy 22 at the time... our local priest at the time, Fr John Doyle had started to play with us that year. He was from Kilmore, played previously with St Peter's College and underage with Wexford. He was one of the mainstays when it came to driving the club forward at the time. He was in corner-back. He continued to play with us for about 10 years and remained involved in the club since.

You can imagine how mad the place was, our first county title ever, and it coming in an All-Ireland year as well.

The next title we won was in '70 with much the same group of players. Fr Martin Casey, a native of Causeway in Kerry, had come into the team at that stage, another man... Michael Jordan, who had missed the final in '68 through injury, had come back into the team again.

Buffers Alley had won two senior championships in three years, but immediately their gallop was stopped in its tracks by Rathnure, who would rule the county for the next four years and would inflict another painful Sunday on their rivals, defeating them in the 1973 final by a goal, 2-7 to 1-7.

The 1970s would be the story of Rathnure and Buffers Alley as, between them, they claimed every senior title apart from one, when Rapparees surprised Rathnure with a three points defeat in 1978.

Rathnure won six titles.

Buffers Alley three.

But, significantly, the black and amber would defeat Tony Doran and Co in two finals (1973 and '77), while Buffers Alley never had the honour of returning the compliment in a county final.

Rathnure had their own two big, strong families, the Quigleys and the O'Connors.

The final in '73... they beat us by a goal in the final... that was a final we often felt hard done by.

I scored a goal about halfway through the second-half but it was brought back for a free... we felt at the time that if it was allowed we might have gone on to win the game.

But we got the free... and got no score. I was clean though and it should not have been brought back.

We went out of the championship in 1971 and '72 a bit unexpected (we were defeated by Ferns and Adamstown in the early rounds), and in '74 Oulart beat us in the semi-final, and Oulart were a major force at that time... and Rathnure went on to beat them in the final.

In '75 we went through to the final fairly easy... Rathnure got beaten in the semi-final by Oulart... so there was a local derby between two neighbours... ourselves and Oulart. They were looking for their first title. I still imagine... of all the finals we were in... that was the biggest build up of all. A lot of us had played together underage previously. Oulart and Buffers Alley had joined in underage and we had won titles at minor and under-21... we played under Buffers Alley when we won a couple of under-21 titles, and played under Oulart when we won a minor title.

Tony Doran, without even a hint of mischief in his voice, but with a smile that perhaps tells a different story, explains that he never got to wear the red and black of the parish to the south.

We would wear each other's jerseys... when you think of the rivalry it is hard to imagine alright... no neutral jerseys. At that time I remember in under-21 we played as Buffers Alley and wore our jerseys. I was never fortunate enough to wear a Oulart jersey.

I was centre-forward in the '75 senior final and playing on Mick Jacob, one of the leading lights in Wexford at the time and a county teammate... and we were tied up family wise because my brother, Bill was full-forward and he was married to Mick's sister, Bridie.

Mick was a great hurler. He was able to take it as strong as the next man, an outstanding hurler.

He hurled and I hurled... but he did a good bit of hurling. I got a few scores. Put it this way, there would have been nothing held back... Mick was one of three Jacob brothers playing on the day, Robbie and Christy were the others. We won by six points. I managed to score 2-2.

Got one early on... their goalie stopped a shot and I was on the follow in and lapped it home... and actually I moved in full-forward when I got the second one... a long ball came in from out the field and I caught it and found the target.

Buffers Alley did most of their damage to Oulart's hopes in the first-half in front of a record attendance (at the time) of 8,500, and held a seven points (2-4 to 0-3) advantage at the change of ends. Oulart turned the tables and with 10 minutes left on the clock had worked themselves into a two-point lead (2-7 to 2-5), but it was Doran's second goal that called halt to any notion that Oulart would actually lift the title. Like everyone else, the Oulart defence knew that they had to stop Doran at all costs, but that task was simply beyond them.

Increasingly, opponents at club and county level knew what to expect from Tony Doran, and they knew that he favoured route one. Stopping him was an entirely different matter, of course.

Most people would tell you that a 'left hand on top hurler' is harder to stop... that most backs play sort of on the left side of a forward... on the left shoulder.

It's probably a disadvantage to be marking a fella with left hand on top because he can shield you away from the ball. Which is what happened with me and Willie Murphy that day... I was shielding the ball to catch it on the other side... and Willie was driving through to get at it.

I always caught the ball in my right hand.... most players normally caught the ball in their left hand... it was just that I was left ha- a certain extent.

When .... striking the ball I would hold the left hand on top of the hurley, as a left hander... most forwards... 95% of players... woul' ' ight hand on top. It's harder for the back to get in... I always found it harder to mark a player who was holding the hurley same as myself because he might be coming from the other side.

But even though I was left handed... and left hand on top... I still would have turned to my right side to strike the ball... most of the time anyhow.

Pa Dillon, the Kilkenny full-back... I played on him quite a lot, and he played the same way I did. Ger Henderson... Kilkenny had quite a number of left handed hurlers... the pure hurler was always regarded as the other type. Another was Jimmy Doyle of Tipperary... he played that way, even though Jimmy struck off the left side most of the time as well.

I did not find a major difference in right and left side, but I turned instinctively towards the right.

A full-back knew that it was safer to stay between Tony Doran and his own goal. In the 1970s and '80s those who occupied the No.3 jersey were more cautious than modern day full-backs.

When we played against Oulart my most regular opponent became Jimmy Prendergast, who played with Wexford at the same time as well... Jimmy was a smaller fella and he would always have been corner back with the county... smaller build, but very wiry, and he had a reputation as being a very good man marker. Sometimes it was better marking bigger men... they had less mobility

If you are in front of a man and you spread yourself it is going to be more difficult for that man to get to the ball, and I had more chance of getting a free in those circumstances as well.

I would spread myself... not doing anything to foul my man... just blocking him from the ball.

Probably one of my strongest assets was catching the ball... and to be on the turn as I caught it... to get a half yard of an advantage on my man... and see if I can get inside him.

In his career with Buffers Alley and Wexford, Tony Doran caught several thousand descending sliotars. But he only suffered two breaks in his career that spanned over three decades. On his left hand he broke his thumb, and also his little finger on the same hand. His right hand, which was responsible for catching all of those balls, was never damaged.

Never had a bruise on the hand I was catching the ball with. People would hardly believe it but that was true.

Beating Oulart The Ballagh in the 1975 county final offered Buffers Alley another chance at All-Ireland glory, but they were denied in Leinster by Kilkenny's James Stephens, who would progress and claim the All-Ireland title. Tony Doran marked a young and very lean Brian Cody that afternoon.

I was playing on Cody that day... it was the first time I played on him. He was only about 21 at the time... slip of a fella. They beat us with a late goal in Wexford Park. He was centre-back and I got a few points off him... but he did a certain amount of hurling as well. I didn't play on him much after that till later in my career

He played full-back with Kilkenny, centre-back, corner-back, left half-back... full-forward for a time... I did not hit up against him in the Leinster Championship till '81 I think it was... when he came in at full-back for Kilkenny as a sub in a semi-final. We won that day, which was the main thing. Probably did alright against him... played against him two years later in Leinster semi-final again.

It was the second disappointment on the national stage for Buffers Alley. In 1971, they had lost to Offaly's St Rynagh's in the provincial final – and that same afternoon was the one and only time in Tony Doran's career that he was sent-off the field of play. Doran was hit with a six months suspension, and Buffers Alley was fined £50, and further deprived of £40 in expenses due from the Leinster Council.

Joe Dooley and I had a bit of an altercation... he was one of my best friends ever since, and he died there recently. It was mostly hand-bag stuff. The game was getting a bit out of hand and Jimmy Hatton, from Wicklow... one of the best referees around in hurling and football at the time, was refereeing it... he needed to stamp it out.

The pair of us got sent off... as a warning to everyone else.

Something happened in the general direction of the ball. It was nothing much... I don't think we struck one another or anything like that. Nothing happened before that either between us... just some jostling.

Six months suspensions seemed to be normal at the time. The chairman of the Leinster Council, Jack Conroy from Laois liked six months... six months, six months, six months... Willie Murphy was sent off in the Leinster final with Wexford at the same time and got six months... for a fairly tame challenge enough.

Six months... Padraig Horan was sent off against Wexford in the Leinster semi-final and got six months. That was the normal thing with the Leinster Council at the time, and if you were up in front of them, you knew what you were getting.

Six months... yah!

Knowing how harsh that suspension was always made me feel for any player hard done by in a disciplinary case.

In 1976, Buffers Alley retained their county title. They defeated Rapparees, 1-11 to 2-4 in the final, and made their way back onto the national stage. It would be another six years before the Alley were again back in Leinster, when in 1982 they won back their county title and further posted a four-in-a-row.

Their third attempt, however, at winning a Leinster and All-Ireland title ended in real tragedy. Once again, Buffers Alley lost one of their own on a Sunday afternoon, and a game of hurling was left looking no longer a matter of 'life and death'.

We got a shock in the first round when we lost to Ardclough, two weeks after the county final... we lost to them in Naas. It was a fully deserved one point win for them... a major surprise, but they had a good team at the time and Kildare had run Wexford close in the Leinster semi-final earlier that year.

On the day of the county final against Rapparees, an officer of the club... Tom Butler, who would have had three nephews on the team, Pierie, Henry and Mick... he dropped dead in the dressing-room at half-time. A lot of players had left the room, but there were still some lads in there when Tom went down. He was in his mid-50s... an awful tragedy for his family... for the club.

The second-half of the game went ahead. Most of the players did not know what happened... but, my brother Joe, he was one of the few players left in the room. He saw Tom falling down, but didn't know what happened fully.

Ironically, it was our second county final win in six years in tragic circumstances.

Buffers Alley winning championships did not bring good tidings to local publicans in Wexford town, or any village on the way home to Monamolin and Kilmuckridge. For starters, none of the Doran boys ever drank alcohol. They were all members of the Pioneer Total Abstinence Association.

Tony Doran remains a Pioneer to this day. His father would have taken a drink on an occasional basis, maybe a couple of bottles of stout if an event in the house really demanded it.

Tony remembers 75% of the Buffers Alley team at that time as being 'non-drinkers'.

Maybe we hadn't the money to drink... I don't know. We did not go down to the local... very seldom... Lawless' in Monamolin. After a county final win it would only be Lucozade or a 7-Up. There was a pub in Enniscorthy which the lads would go into after a county final too, and the owner would say to everyone that when Buffers Alley were playing he would have to get in an extra supply of Club Orange.

That's what he said more than once.

Neither did the team indulge in too much coaching.

There were six selectors at work when Buffers Alley won their first senior county title in 1968, and two years later that number was cut back to three men. Officially there was no manager, no coach.

I suppose Ger Dempsey was one of the figureheads who would do most of the training and take it... and Fr John Doyle would have done a certain amount of it when he was playing too after coaching teams in St Peter's.

Training moved around between different men... but Ger Dempsey was the main one... we trained Tuesday and Thursday... maybe Tuesday and Friday some weeks... but no session before a match.

Jesus no... we usually finished on the Tuesday night before a match and did nothing for the rest of the week

Usually Tuesday or Wednesday... Monday or Wednesday would be the last session before a big game.

Ger Dempsey felt you had to be fresh... and that it was far more important to be fresh. Ger was into greyhounds as well and I think he believed in training us like greyhounds. You had to have the greyhound fresh... and you had to have men fresh.

It was a whole different game back then... I suppose at the start at county level the training consisted of a few laps of the field and then sprints... little bit of physical exercise, but nothing major. There was no question of gyms at the time, or anything that even looked like a gymnasium.

I remember our first county final in 1968 was played in the depths of winter (December 8)... and in the hall in Monamolin... we would tog out in the hall and do our training in a field at the back of the hall.

We'd be up to our ankles in mud... and we'd probably work away in the mud for half an hour... maybe 35 minutes... that was the training.

No ball work... that would be left to the Sunday.

When we won in 1970 things had progressed a bit, and in the field where we hurled across the road from our home place a good few of the lads who farmed or were self-employed... or working say in Enniscorthy or whatever... we'd start our training at three o'clock in the day. Lads might get off work a bit early and get an hour's training in while there was still some light in the day.

I recall one day while training for the 1970 county final we had this three o'clock session and we were togging out in an old grain *loft at home. Now, anyone with farming experience at that time can imagine what that loft was like!*

Just as about 20 of us were coming down the steps of the loft, to cross the road for training, a car had pulled up outside, and as the occupant was getting out he was nearly trampled by the lot of us who had only one thing on our minds. I'd imagine the person in the car might have wished the ground to open up and swallow him. It turned out it was Jim Whitney, an official of Shamrocks who were playing us in the final. He was calling into our house in his work as an ESB employee.

In 1977, Buffers Alley were beaten in the county final by Rathnure. It was a day in which the rain spilled, and continued to spill without much thought, and while it was touch and go for a long time, Rathnure were three points to the good at the end. The following year they went out in the semi-final to Rapparees, who went on to win the county title. In '79, Gorey, who were not considered a major threat, beat the Alley by half a dozen points. It was Rathnure's title in '79.

Then, in 1980, it was Buffers Alley and Rathnure back in a county final once more in Wexford Park, and most neutrals presumed that the Alley would have their day at last against their toughest of opponents. But it was not so.

Rathnure won easily.

A thundering 2-15 to 1-7.

When Buffers Alley won their way back to the final against Faythe Harriers 12 months later, they did so after beating Rathnure in the semi-final. Again, it was expected that the Alley would have their day, but a last minute goal helped the Harriers to nick it at the very end by a single point. It was revenge for what the Alley had done to them in 1968.

Tony Doran was 35 years-old.

Time to be thinking of retirement, surely?

Not really... I suppose we were still thinking of winning... and I was still playing with Wexford at that stage as well.

We went on.

Buffers Alley went on to win four-in-a-row… '82, '83, '84 and '85!

I was not covering the same ground as a few years before… my game changed a certain amount. In '81 we were favourites to win the championship the whole year, and we beat Rathnure in the semi-final… the Harriers caught us in the final.

There were so many good teams in the county and very little difference between any of us when it came down to a big day.

In '82 and '83 Fr Jim Butler was training the team, and he had three brothers on the team as well. He was in St Peter's at the time, I think… he was recently ordained and younger than most of us on the team. Young fellas in the club had gone through Peter's with him and he had some success with underage teams in the club. He followed onto the senior team and did a fantastic job with us. He pulled out of it then and my brother Colm took up the training in '84 and '85.

In 1982 Buffers Alley defeated Oulart (1-9 to 1-6), in '83 they saw off St Martin's (1-13 to 1-11), and in '84 after a replay (2-5 to 0-5) and '85 (1-14 to 0-12) they got the better of Faythe Harriers.

Tony Doran was about to turn 40 years of age.

In those years, after we won the county title, the big thing was to win the Leinster title. St Rynagh's beat us by three points in the Leinster final in '82… we were beaten in a semi-final, after a replay, by Portlaoise in '83, and St Martin's of Kilkenny beat us in '84… again in a semi-final.

In 1985 we won our first Leinster title in some style… beat Kinnity of Offaly, 3-9 to 0-7. It was their third Leinster final in-a-row to lose, and they had five Allstars on their team at the time. We played very well… beat them well in Nowlan Park.

I got on reasonably well.

Got a couple of goals anyhow, so I didn't do too badly.

We had a mixture of a lot of young fellas… all in their early

20s, and we had few old stagers as well... a good mix... lads with good heads. Colm was still playing corner-back and he was 36 at the time... I was there... 39... Henry Butler, better known as 'Har', in our goal was 37... Mick Butler was 35 in corner-forward, and Martin Casey was wing forward or midfield and he was also 35.

But the majority of the others were in their early- to mid-20s.

Buffers Alley defeated Cushendall (1-10 to 0-5) in the 1985 All-Ireland semi-final, and at last got to walk onto the greatest stage in the club game when they met Kilruane McDonaghs of Tipperary in Croke Park on St Patrick's Day.

Buffers Alley lost by two points.

1-15 to 2-10.

Tony Doran felt that he was only 'middling' on the greatest day in the club's history up to that point. He got a couple of scores, but he needed to do more if Buffers Alley was to become the single greatest club team in the country.

Back home in Wexford, in the county final in 1986, Buffers Alley were stopped in their tracks by Rathnure, losing by five points, as they sought to make it five in-a-row in the county for the first time.

It always seemed to be Rathnure who ruined the greatest of days.

In 1987, Rathnure got the better of Buffers Alley in the county semi-final. Then, in 1988, Buffers Alley fought their way through to the county final again. There they met Rathnure.

And Buffers Alley had never beaten Rathnure when it mattered more than anything else. They did not beat them on October 16, 1988 either. Rathnure dominated from the opening whistle and they still looked untouchable when they led by double scores early in the second-half. It was then that Tony Doran had his wits about him and grabbed a life-saving goal. Within a minute, the Alley almost got a second goal, but Mick Butler's shot came back off the bar. It was Paddy Donohoe who scored the Alley's second goal, and within 60 seconds Paul Gahan took his point from a free far out the field. The teams, sensationally, were level.

Rathnure forged ahead a second time, but Butler then struck a 21-yard free low and hard, and hopping, to the back of the net. Butler then had a rasping shot saved by John Conran, before referee Dickie Murphy sounded the final whistle 60 seconds too early.

It was the sixth time they had failed to fell the men from the west of the county.

It was a drawn match.

Rathnure 2-14, Buffers Alley 3-11.

They would meet a week later, back in Wexford Park, for the replay. For seven days Tony Doran and those around him had to work out in their heads how and why they always seemed to find Rathnure a hurdle too high.

A week later Buffers Alley would take the victory the club so craved…

Chapter 1

It was nearly always Kilkenny.

From the very beginning, it seemed that there was no other way forward. If Tony Doran wanted to do anything as a Wexford hurler, win anything at all, Kilkenny came first.

There was no escape from them.

The black and amber was always there, strong, forceful, arrogant most of the time, but rightly so. They expected to beat Wexford.

As though it was their duty.

Therefore, Tony Doran would meet on the field of play – usually directly in front of the Kilkenny goalmouth – the best and most devout of full-backs. Over the course of three decades, he would meet them all… the likes of Pa Dillon, Nicky Orr, Paddy Prendergast, Brian Cody… others who came before them, or in between them, and some who came after them. Nobody met more Kilkenny full-backs. Occasionally he scorched them. Now and then they battled courageously and overcame him. All of them, however, were greater men for having taken on Tony Doran.

He would win.

He would also be beaten down on certain days, but by the end of his career, Kilkenny hurling folk would remember the name Tony Doran. They would come to salute him, recognise him as someone who caused greater damage to Kilkenny's All-Ireland cause than any other hurler in the 1960s, 70s, and 80s.

Doran, in fact, helped to make Kilkenny great.

Not that he ever wished.

And, indeed, at the very beginning of his remarkable career, there was no indication whatsoever that he, and the Wexford teams on which he was chosen, would ever have to bend a knee to their imperious neighbours.

The first time he came face-to-face with Kilkenny on Ireland's greatest stage was the 1963 Leinster minor hurling final. There were 12 goals in the game. The game of hurling was more bloodthirsty in the 60s and goals were always in demand. Tony Doran remembers Wexford hitting seven goals past Laois in the Leinster semi-final. He got four of them himself. And, of course, in the All-Ireland final, Tony Doran claimed his first All-Ireland medal when Wexford overcame Limerick. The score?

Wexford 6-12, Limerick 5-9.

Winning seemed easy, and winning by putting up big numbers of goals in Croke Park appeared the natural order of things.

You start to think like that, but it didn't happen.

It was a big score against Kilkenny in the minor final. All of the games at that time had fairly high scoring. In the All-Ireland final we beat Limerick and got six more.

But we never expected to have it easy against Kilkenny... not like that. I can barely remember a bad Kilkenny defence... when they just weren't at the races. Kilkenny were Kilkenny... they were the team I came up against all my career really. In Leinster they were the regular team to beat in all grades.

In the Leinster minor final, in '63... I have certain memories.

For some reason it was played not on the same day as the senior final... it was played a week or two afterwards. For whatever reason, I can't remember. My memory of it is that we had a fairly good lead for most of the match and in the first-half we ran up a big lead of 12... or 15 points, but just typical Kilkenny... they came back at us in the second-half and we just held on for our win.

There was a certain psychological barrier there for Wexford, because we had never won a Leinster minor... never won it, ever.

There was no reason for that, it was just how it was. Wexford contested finals then in the 1950s and early 60s, and eventually we got over the line against Kilkenny in '63.

There was a certain amount of belief that we could win it in '63. There was an expectation. St Peter's College were doing really well... they'd won an All-Ireland colleges around that same period and other schools in Wexford were also doing fairly well. So there was a strong belief there, but we still had to get over the line and actually beat Kilkenny in a first Leinster final.

We would have that 'thing' about Kilkenny but as young lads we didn't think they were unbeatable at the time. I don't think anything like that was in our minds... we just felt that we had a game to play and we felt that we could win it.

I was playing centre-forward most of the time, but also moving between centre and full-forward.

I got three goals.

Lucky enough.

I suppose I had a certain instinct for scoring goals... maybe a little bit too much so... when I should have being taking my points.

But I tended to look for goals.

Limerick were the clear favourites in the 1963 All-Ireland minor final. They had more or less marched through a more fearsome Munster championship. Wexford were strictly in the 'underdog' role.

But we would have thought we had a chance.

Limerick had a good few big names that became even bigger names in the years after that. Eamonn Cregan was their standout player. We'd have heard about him... playing down there and playing colleges... we'd have heard a good bit about him.

In the early 60s teams did not know all that much about their opponents, and did not seek to further their knowledge. Mainly, there was just talk, most of it 'big talk' sourced from the grape vine, and therefore not all that reliable. There was no television, no radio – no DVD's, God forbid. There was nobody heading down south on spying missions. Nobody climbing trees.

It was a time of trust, and innocence.

None of us on the team would ever have seen Eamonn Cregan play, and I'd doubt if anyone in Wexford would have seen him either... any of the mentors over the team.

We were definitely going in blind... and maybe on what we had read in the papers, if there was anything about the minor match in the papers. At that stage team mentors did not go and look at other teams. It was the last thing people thought of doing at that time back then.

It was a fairly see-saw affair in the final. Both teams had their periods of dominance and one would go ahead and it was only in the last minutes that we took over and got a few scores and opened up daylight.

I got two goals.

He remembers travelling up to Dublin on the morning of the game by car. There were four or five lads living in the east of the county who were on the Wexford panel. One of the team selectors based in Ferns, Paddy Brosnan was in the car and Tommy Cahill also from Ferns was the driver. Mick Kinsella, Freddie Swords and Conor O'Rafferty were also in the car.

Where I was living and with nobody else in the club involved, I was a little bit out on a limb on my own... some games I'd travel with some of the lads from the Enniscorthy area, because they had room. John Murphy was their car driver. I went up to the Leinster final with them.

We stopped off at the International Hotel in Bray. For All-Ireland weekends at the time that was the Wexford base, near the seafront... that was where Wexford teams always stayed for big weekends... for ordinary games we went to the Phoenix Hotel on Parkgate Street.

The Phoenix wasn't five star or anything... we didn't do five star. That's where Wexford teams of that time from all grades went, except for All-Irelands... then we'd go to the International... and stay overnight.

Jerseys were nearly always used before. I wouldn't say they were ever new. Only recently, a friend of mine told me that his father played minor with Wexford in the 50s and he remembered coming in off the field in Nowlan Park after playing minor for the county in a championship game... and he had to give his jersey to the senior player who was playing in the same position as him.

The senior team was waiting to wear the same jerseys. People today would hardly believe that.

It was a different time, but I think... an easier time.

I can't even be sure if we even got shorts for that All-Ireland final in '63. I think we might have been wearing our own shorts that we'd been wearing all year. Very possibly... we did get socks... because prior to that everyone had different coloured socks. There was no question of all of us having the same coloured socks.

A hurler, or a footballer back then... you did not have half a dozen pairs of socks at any one time. You'd have the one pair of socks... and you'd wear them until there was hardly anything left in them.

I remember we did get a new pair of socks for that All-Ireland final... because it was a big deal for all us, a new pair of socks that we'd have for the whole of the next year... I don't think we got the togs.

That was a big thing... a big deal then.

Oh yeah, that was about it. We got that pair of socks for the All-Ireland minor final and I'd say, possibly, the next pair of socks

I got in a Wexford dressing-room was for the senior final in 1968. That was just how it was.

As regards togs... I'd say we didn't get a new pair of Wexford togs until then as well. We never got anything when we were in under-21 championship finals... possibly because those games were usually played away from Croke Park.

The first time I ever got to keep a Wexford jersey after a match was after the 1968 All-Ireland final. And that was a bit of a surprise, I think, that we were allowed to keep them... it was the first Wexford jersey I ever owned.

Jerseys would be thrown in by players, as soon as they arrived back into the dressing-room after games. They would be counted out on a wooden table in the middle of the room to make sure that all of them – including the subs – had been returned after every match.

If you played for Leinster in a Railway Cup, you'd get to keep the jersey... and togs and socks... the whole lot... that was an extra big prize. That was a big thing in the 60s.

Oh yeah, definitely. There surely was no question of ever seeing a tracksuit.

There was a fella in Wexford, called Bill Peare, who was there all of the time. He was from Enniscorthy. Bill was the regular kit man and he was worth his weight in gold to the county board. Bill was a very decent fella... but Bill's top job was to make sure all the jerseys were in the bag after the match.

He'd mind those jerseys with his life.

He'd bring them home and wash them all. County boards were working off a much tighter budget then. There was nobody sponsoring anything then... jerseys or tracksuits... nothing.

Kilkenny defeated Waterford in the All-Ireland senior final in Croke Park the same day in 1963. It was a whopping 4-17 to 6-8 for the Cats. During the minor final, the crowd was still assembling. Neither group of supporters had a vested interest in the warm-up game.

Tony Doran was the only Buffers Alley man on the Wexford minor panel in '63, but it was a dressing-room made up of characters and 'big names', and lads who believed they had a lifetime of adventure in the purple and gold ahead of them in their adult lives. Sixteen year-old Liam Byrne was goalkeeper, with John Hartley, Mick Nolan and Eamonn O'Connor in the full-back line. The half-backs were Vinny Staples and Mick Kinsella and Joe Murphy. The three of them would advance to the senior team. Murphy would win a National League with Wexford... but eventually he'd head off to Australia. In the middle of the field, from Wexford town, was Willie Bernie who was also the team captain. Bernie was one of the 'big names' on the team, even though he never got to have a lengthy career in the Wexford colours owing to ill health. Gorey's Conor Rafferty was his midfield partner. In the forward line was Con Dowdall from Faythe Harriers, Seamus Barron, Pat Quigley from Rathnure, Willie Carley from Na Fianna and Freddie Swords from Riverchapel.

Mick Kinsella was the only other Buffers Alley man, I suppose you'd have to say... Mick was born in our area, in Kilmuckridge, but his father was a teacher and moved to Gorey to work, and Mick played with Gorey at that time. Then a couple of years after that he came back to us... so he was a Buffers Alley man even though he wasn't a Buffers Alley man in '63.

We put a bit of pressure on him to come back to us, and he did... I'm very happy to say.

I was minor again the following year. But we were beaten in the first round in Leinster by Kilkenny. We had seven or eight of the previous year's team and we thought we were going to be freewheeling again... but... it didn't happen. One game.

That was it.

Kilkenny were always there... ready to spoil the party.

In *The Irish Times* on September 2, 1963, it fell to their young but already venerable GAA writer, Paddy Downey to deliver his thoughts on Wexford's 6-12 to 5-9 victory over Limerick. Downey, like his colleagues of the day, was a wordsmith who was never shy about throwing himself into the thick of the action. In getting his hands around the final stages of the game, he delivered it thus:

'... Instead of cracking under the pressure, however, Wexford surged back on the attack, and Willie Bernie, who had been strangely inconspicuous until then, burst on the scene with two brilliantly taken goals, which really broke the back of the Limerick resistance.

With the Munster boys' challenge virtually spent, the tempo dropped considerably in the last quarter, and while Con Danaher hit back with a late Limerick goal, the effort was of no more than token importance, and Wexford quickly righted themselves to run out convincing winners.

On a well-balanced Wexford team, which should prove a tremendous boost to the county's hurling fortunes, John Hartley and Michael Kinsella got through a tremendous amount of work in defence, but the real stylist of the sector was Vincent Staples, who capped a magnificent display at left half-back with a spectacular goal from 90 yards' range early in the second-half.

Bernie, who captained the team at midfield, left a big imprint on the game in the second-half, while the pick of the clever, quick-pulling attack were Tony Doran, Seamus Barron and Con Dowdall.

Eamonn Cregan was a dynamic force at midfield for Limerick, but apart from John Egan, Tom McAuliffe, Tony Roche and Bernie Savage, the necessary support wasn't forthcoming to offset Wexford's great all-round strength.

Wexford: *L Byrne; J Hartley, M Nolan, E O'Connor; J Murphy, M Kinsella, V Staples (1-1); W Bernie (2-0), C Rafferty; C Dowdall (0-8 from frees), A Doran (2-1), F Swords (0-1); W Carley (0-1), S Barron (1-0), P Quigley. Sub: B Gaule for Hartley.*
Limerick: *A Dunworth; S O'Brien, J Egan, S O'Shaughnessy; P Heffernan, T McAuliffe, P O'Brien; A Roche (0-6 from frees), E Cregan (0-1); C Danaher (1-0), B Savage (0-2), M Graham; S Geary (1-0), G Cosgrave (1-0), B Cobbs (2-0).*

Life as a Wexford hurler seemed so grand.

The county's recent history from a decade earlier, when Nickey Rackard and his merry men won the approval and respect of the whole country with back-to-back All-Ireland senior victories, had opened a door that was massively wide.

Wexford were All-Ireland minor champions in 1963. They would claim the same prize again in '66 and '68.

I suppose there was a crop of players, and we were competitive at underage. We won the All-Ireland at under-21 in '65... we'd reached the final in '64 and again in '66, won three in-a-row in Leinster. I'd say that was the nucleus of the 1968 All-Ireland winning team... with a few survivors off the Wexford team from the early part of the decade.

We beat Dublin in the Leinster under-21 final '65... we'd beaten Kilkenny in the first round. We'd actually beaten Kilkenny at under-21 in '64... beat them again in '65 and '66. We had a bit over them for those few years in the Leinster championship.

Our own Joe was midfield for Wexford in that winning under-21 final, which made it doubly special, and the same year Bill, Joe and myself were on the Wexford Intermediate team that was beaten by Cork in the All-Ireland 'Home' final. That was another proud day for our family.

For four years, Tony Doran represented Wexford at the under-21 grade. And, like his days as a minor in the purple and gold, he got the ultimate return for time served by being part of an All-Ireland winning team in 1965.

Wexford saw off Kilkenny in the first round in 1964, in New Ross, by 4-3 to 2-5. There was a big win over Dublin next, in a game in which Tony Doran says he was 'fortunate enough' to score six goals. Included in the Dublin team were faces who would soon become famous for playing the bigger ball – Jimmy Keaveney, Tony Hanahoe and Gay O'Driscoll – and who would win three All-Ireland senior titles as part of Kevin Heffernan's brilliant Dublin team of the 1970s. There was another big win over Laois, and another over Antrim in the All-Ireland semi-final followed, before their march was stopped in its tracks, very early in the All-Ireland final in Nowlan Park, when Tipperary crushed Wexford 8-9 to 3-1. Doran missed the semi-final due to injury, and lost his place for the final.

And in 1966, as the Wexford team set about its defence of their Leinster and

All-Ireland under-21 titles, they took Kilkenny out of it in a Leinster semi-final in Enniscorthy, 6-11 to 2-0. It was one of Wexford's most commanding days of all time over their vaunted neighbours. Antrim, in the All-Ireland semi-final in Belfast, were also blitzed, and it took three matches against Cork before it was decided who would be crowned 1966 All-Ireland under-21 champs.

Wexford 5-6, Cork 3-12 (Nowlan Park, Kilkenny).

Wexford 4-9, Cork 4-9 (Gaelic Grounds, Limerick).

Wexford 5-9, Cork 9-9 (Croke Park).

In between, in 1965 Tony Doran and Co in turn defeated Wicklow 17-9 to 0-0, Kilkenny (5-7 to 5-3), Offaly (3-5 to 2-3), Dublin (7-9 to 1-5), Antrim (8-13 to 0-4), and finally in the deciding game of the championship, Tipperary (3-7 to 1-4). It was pretty much plain sailing apart from slipping by Kilkenny by four points and Offaly by five points early in the campaign. A total of 43 goals in six games reveals the simplicity of Wexford's tactical planning.

Wexford adapted best to the awful weather conditions in Nowlan Park in the 1965 final, when one of their primary jobs was to nullify the threat of Babs Keating, which they did, limiting the lethal attacker to a single goal from a 40 yards free.

Tipperary were favourites for that final in '65. But we had a very strong team at the time. We'd been beaten in the '65 senior final... Tipp had beaten the seniors the week before... and both teams had a fair sprinkling from the senior final playing in the under-21 final.

Mick Jacob was in goals for us, and in front of him there was Willie O'Neill, Dan Quigley and Aidan Somers. Vinny Staples, Mick Kinsella and Willie Murphy were our half-backs, and Joe had Eugene Ryan from St Patrick's with him in the middle of the field. Con Dowdall, Pat Quigley and Seamus Barron were the half-forwards, and either side of me at full-forward were Tony Maher and Jack Berry. Christy Jacob came on as a sub in that final.

Cork, the following year in 66? Went to three games... they won pretty well in the end on the third day. Cork in that final scored as many goals as points... nine goals. But it was a final we were capable of winning. I was team captain, which was a double disappointment to eventually lose it.

In the previous two drawn games we were caught at the death by Cork in both of them... and to lose the third day was fierce hard to take. First game was in Nowlan Park... second in Limerick and third in Croker... we had a good tour around the country over those five or six weeks.

They had a lot of big names on their team at that time because a number of them had also won the senior All-Ireland with Cork. It was a young Cork team that came from nowhere to win the All-Ireland... in '66... you had the McCarthys... the three of them, and Seanie Barry was there as well, their free-taker and scorer-in-chief.

Justin McCarthy was their stand-out player at the time, but Charlie McCarthy was in corner-forward and he was special... Gerald McCarthy had captained Cork to the senior all-Ireland... just 21 he was. They had other fellas too, all very well known.

Justin was a very stylish player and he was one of those who would always catch your eye... stand out, even at that time when he was only 21. I suppose he was unlucky that a few years later in a road accident he received very severe injuries. He came back and played again, but that setback put a dampener on his career... he was only 24 at the time... coming into his prime.

They were training for an All-Ireland in '69, when he had the accident. He did not play for a few years after that. They felt at the time that he might never play again, but he came back with Cork in the early 70s, but probably never got back to where he was... maybe that is how he got into the coaching and became very successful there also.

The third and final game in the epic series against Cork in 1966 was presented in *The Irish Times* by Peter Byrne thus:

'A scoreline of 9-9 to 5-9 conveys little of the drama and excitement which, for 45 minutes, made this second replay of the under-21 final one of the finest hurling games seen at Croke Park in years.

In the end, Cork won readily enough, but the abiding memory which the vast majority of spectators will have taken away from the game will surely not be of Wexford's last-quarter collapse, but rather the velvet quality of the hurling, which far surpassed anything in the senior final.

True, a total of 14 goals in any game hints of defensive mistakes. And there were errors, to be sure, on a murky afternoon, when it took a sharp eye to trace the flight of the ball.

But even the November gloom could not cloak the brilliance of some of the forward play, as Cork, in particular, plotted the goals which kept the scoreboard men working at a brisk pace throughout the entire hour.

At half-time there was every reason to anticipate another cliff-hanging finish as Wexford hit back from a couple of nervy patches to trail by only a point, 2-4 to 1-6, when the teams reappeared for the second-half.

A quick point by Eddie Cousins balanced the scoring in the 32nd minute, but then Cork made the first big breakthrough, which was to spell doom for the Leinster champions' hopes.

Four minutes after the interval a ground shot by Charlie McCarthy appeared to pose no particular problems for the Wexford defence but with the goalkeeper, Henry Butler, unsighted, the full-forward, Andy Flynn, doubled the ball to the net.

Points by Charlie McCarthy and Sean Barry (2) followed and with the southerners in a clear-cut five points lead, it looked as if the Wexford challenge had spent itself. But the signs were proved wrong in the 42nd minute when Seamus Barron lashed home a 21 yards free and the losers were back in the game with a chance.

Eddie O'Brien had a Cork goal in the 46th minute after Barry's shot had been only partially cleared but with characteristic grit, Wexford surged back for one of the best goals of the game when Tony Doran first-timed Barron's free to the net.

Everything, it seemed, was now set for a fourth meeting to determine the destination of the trophy but, just as suddenly, the floodgates opened on the Wexford goal. In the last ten minutes with the losers rapidly running out of steam, Charlie McCarthy (2), Peter Curley (2), and O'Brien went through for goals which made a mockery of Wexford's courageous stand earlier on.

In apportioning the individual honours, one was impressed by the utter reliability of the Cork defence in which the goalkeeper John Mitchell, Jack Russell and Denis Coughlan were the dominant figures. But the chief inspiration for this splendid win *surely stemmed from the magnificent display of Justin McCarthy, whose long-range striking and general industry around the centre of the field must have broken the hearts of the Wexford supporters.'*

Cork never did take it easy on us.

They'd beat us in three senior finals in my time... and beat us in that under-21 final in '66. They also beat Wexford in three in-a-row of under-21 finals in '69, '70, '71... the only big win we had over them was in minor finals in '66 and '68.

It shouldn't have been a big deal about playing Cork, but they became a certain amount of a bogey team at that time.

To lose to them in three senior finals in eight years... I don't know? There was no great reason for it that we could see. We were able to beat them in the other games... in the league... but they beat us in the National league final in '69 alright... but, any other games, we could beat them.

We just could not get over the line against them in All-Ireland finals. There was no particular reason for it... not one... genuinely, not that I can think of.

As he was representing Buffers Alley, the honour of captaining his county fell to Tony Doran in that All-Ireland under-21 final defeat to Cork in 1966, and also in the back-to-back All-Ireland senior final defeats to 'The Rebels' in 1976 and '77.

Each time, however, Tony Doran did not get to accept the cup on behalf of the people of Wexford, and he didn't get to say a word – not that Tony Doran had ever prepared a speech before a final in which he captained Wexford.

The only national trophy he received as a Wexford captain was the All-Ireland Masters (Over-40s) cup in 1991. He kept his speech to a few short sentences.

The way it fell at that time, the county champions nominated the captain. The first time I captained Wexford was in '69... got beaten in the first round... so I haven't a good record as captain.

I was also captain in '71, and again in '83.

I never looked at being captain as some form of big deal... obviously it is an honour, especially when you get to an All-Ireland final. But I never found it a big thing.

Captains in our day never had an awful lot to say. In my early days with Wexford the county chairman was the man who did the talking in the room. He was the one... at minor, under-21, senior... he was the man who did the talking. He was Sean Browne... Sean was chairman all through that time.

He was a TD at the time... and he could talk.

The first time I can remember anyone else talking... a team mentor or anything was when we had Padge Keogh in charge of us in '68. He took over a certain amount of it at that stage... and Padge could talk to lads, no problem there either.

Ned Power did all of the team training at minor and under-21, and senior also. Ned was a Kilkenny man from Slieverue... Ned was a very popular fella with all the lads, but Ned was a man of few words when it came to talking in public or anything like that.

He'd very seldom say anything in public. He'd say his piece in private alright... but he was not a man to push himself forward.

First time I played with Wexford at minor level... we were in the old dressing-rooms in Croke Park... tucked under the Cusack Stand. The dressing-room where the minors were was only tiny sure... hardly room to breathe in.

Sean Browne would start talking and the first thing he did was read out the team...

GOALIE...

RIGHT CORNER-BACK...

FULL-BACK...

LEFT CORNER-BACK...

And sure everyone would have to line up in their position in the dressing room... in the middle of the floor, in that tiny room. That was the thing... we'd all be lined up. And that was how it was still done when I first started to play senior with Wexford.

Browne would say his few words then... while we were all standing in our position.

Chapter 2

Tony Doran got to sit in the senior Wexford dressing-room for the first time in 1964. It was a tournament game, in New Ross. Appropriately enough, considering all of the mighty battles he would have with his nearest and fiercest neighbours over the course of the next three decades, it was Kilkenny who provided the opposition that afternoon. Doran was 17 years-old.

In his own words he calls this early introduction to the seniors as him 'hanging around' the team.

I don't know why I was playing.

I was centre-forward that day. A lot of fellas from the 50s and early 60s were still there at the time... y'know... Ned Wheeler, Billy Rackard... lads like that, all of those were still there at the time. I had scored a few goals at minor and they must have thought I was going to do the same at senior level but... God... I was out of my depth.

Quite naturally, I disappeared off the radar quite quickly after that.

I got on the ball very little that first day... I wasn't fit for it at all... strength-wise, ability-wise, head-wise... in any way, I wasn't ready for that level of hurling.

Next time I got a run with the seniors was, more or less, from late '65 on... I became a regular. I did not play championship till '67, but I played league, Walsh Cup, Oireachtas... all of those. Immediately after the under-21 All-Ireland in '65 we had gone to Kilkenny for an Oireachtas semi-final and I was more or less a regular from then on.

I won my first medal with Wexford at senior level when we beat Kilkenny in the Walsh Cup final at Wexford Park in October of 1965. The same day I scored my first goal for the Wexford senior team.

When it came to the 1966 championship, however, Tony Doran's name was not included on the Wexford senior panel. It was never explained to him why he was dropped. He had played through the league campaign 1965-66, and in May of '66 he was thought good enough to make the trip to London, for the annual Wembley tournament games.

It was his first time to walk out onto the most famous turf in English football history, and where a few months later Alf Ramsey and Bobby Moore would lead their country to victory in the World Cup, getting by West Germany 4-1 in the final after extra-time as centre-forward Geoff Hurst struck his memorable hat-trick. In May of that same year Wexford had met Cork at Wembley Stadium, and Tony Doran was a substitute, but he was sent into the action for the last 20 minutes of the game.

He scored a goal and a point in his limited time on the field.

That was the way it happened... Wembley to bust in 1966 for me!

But I got to play in Wembley a few times after that. It was good craic at the time. A big thing it was too... to get a breakaway at that time in Ireland... even to London for a weekend was a big deal.

There would be, I don't know... but maybe there was 40,000 people there in the stadium for those games... at least, I'd say. I was back in Wembley nearly every year, for the next four or five years, but you could see the crowds getting smaller.

We always flew over... something I didn't like... never liked flying... and don't like yet. Never took to it.

The footballers and hurlers... we stayed in the same hotel. They weren't five star maybe, but they were alright. They wouldn't want to have been five star with the shenanigans going on with fellas anyhow. Of course, on the Allstar tours to America we always stayed with families in whatever city we were visiting... Boston, Chicago... San Francisco.

The following year, in 1967, there was nobody doubting Tony Doran's place on the Wexford team. He was 21 years-old, just about, when he was back in Croke Park and winning again. He picked up his first National league medal. Wexford were too good for Kilkenny in the final, winning with something to spare, 3-10 to 1-9.

It was never easy against Kilkenny, God no, but beating them was becoming a habit for Wexford teams in which Tony Doran took his place.

The league campaign of 1966/67 started off in November, in New Ross against Kilkenny when Wexford won by six points (3-5 to 0-8), but the Cats avenged that loss at the latter half of the same campaign, in Nowlan Park in a play-off game, when they won by two points (2-9 to 3-4). In between, Wexford had defeated Laois, Offaly and Waterford, but had received a right thumping in Thurles from Tipperary, 4-12 to 1-3.

Wexford won their way through all the same to the semi-final where they ran riot against Limerick (6-12 to 1-11), but when Jimmy O'Brien led them out against defending champions, Kilkenny for the final on May 29 they were still written off as rank outsiders by all of the writing giants in the national newspapers.

Amongst those giants with their notebooks and pens was Paddy Downey of *The Irish Times*, who ate his humble pie the morning after the match, but did so with his customary lofty style:

'The critics (this writer included) this morning breakfast, quite appropriately, on the headlines of last week. And there are no questions: because there was none

at Croke Park yesterday when Wexford scored a fully merited seven-point win over Kilkenny, the holders and almost unanimous favourites, in the final of the National Hurling League.

With hindsight it can now be said that Wexford's fine performance in the semi-final against Limerick should have been seen for what it was – the signal that the selectors' long process of team building, the blending of young and seasoned players, had at last succeeded.

There was no doubt about it yesterday as the smooth-moving Wexford side, striking with speed and power, proceeded to hammer the title-holders in the last 20 minutes of the game.

It had been a close battle, embellished with skilful hurling, throughout the first-half and for eight minutes of the second. Scores abnormally low because of defensive vigilance had been level five times (thrice in the first-half) and the tally stood at 1-3 each at the break. Superficially it seemed that the pendulum would continue to swing the inch either way right up to a nerve-wracking finish...'

It turned out that the attendance of 23,109 were not left on the edges of their seats through that second-half. Wexford replaced Fergus Duff with Christy Jacob at the start of the second period at right full-forward – and he was not at all slow to leave his mark on the game. In the 38th minute Phil Wilson, who was completely dominant over Seamus Cleere, dropped a 50 yards lob into the Kilkenny goalmouth. Ollie Walsh jumped close to the right post to stop the ball, but it broke to his left and with the rest of the Kilkenny defence caught ball-watching, Jacobs was in like a light to crack the sliotar to the back of the net.

It was like a switch was flicked, as every single Wexfordman stepped up to a higher level. The defence pulled the shutters down. In the middle of the field Joe Murphy and Dick Shannon were in complete command all of a sudden. A third Wexford goal was on the cards, and they did not lie. In the 45th minute a Paul Lynch free was stopped, but Tony Doran was first to react and struck the sliotar to the net.

Wexford would have only three wides in the second-half, whereas, Kilkenny, trying too hard to haul down the deficit, erred eight times when shooting from relatively close range and only Eddie Keher (eight points to his name by the close of play) really threatened right to the very end. Kilkenny had 15 wides over the hour, compared to Wexford's economical eight. Each of Wexford's six starting forwards got his name on the scoreboard,

For us, beating Kilkenny was a big thing... it still was. That was the start of a reasonably good run we had against Kilkenny... for four or five years after that, but then the wheel turned and it went the other way. I had played against them a few times... Walsh Cup, Oireachtas, National league matches in the two years before that and we had always done reasonably well.

Coming up against Kilkenny was always the biggest ultimate adventure, no matter who had won the last match between us... our next door neighbours... our closest rivals... sure we played them nearly every year in Leinster... underage, senior... they were always there.

There was no avoiding them.

It was a huge thing at the time, and beating them in a national final was something rare... and wonderful for us.

The first regular Kilkenny opponent I had was Pa Dillon who had been there a few years before me. He would have been their most regular full-back at the time.

He was a tough man.

Old style in how he played the game, big time... though I got on fairly well with Pa... even though Pa would have been a tough customer... he was an old style full-back who at that time had as his first job to make sure that the forwards did not get in near their goalkeeper.

Pa would mind the front of the Kilkenny goal with his life. As a stick man I think he was under-rated also because he was a great man for the flicks... getting the ball out of danger... and I think he was a good ball player... very under-rated.

He was known as a tough customer on the edge of the square, but he had a lot more going for him than that.

Like all full-backs at that stage, if Pa did not mind his

goalkeeper properly he would have people to answer to back in his own dressing-room. It was still a few years, don't forget, before forwards were stopped from touching the goalie in possession... there was no rule to protect the goalie, and because of that he was game for anything before then.

The full-back, as you see in old photographs from any matches back in the 60s, is always there close to his goalkeeper, as are most of the other backs in those photographs... with their hurls up and banging them into the chests of whatever number of forwards are also around the square... to keep them out.

That was a regular thing. At that time exchanges would have been fairly hot and heavy around the goalmouth area... there was so much action going on around that area that goals were more plentiful.

Maybe that was because we were playing with a slower ball, I don't know... but the sliotar was made that way at the time... it was heavier than it is now. The ball would end up in the square a lot... and would end up in the net a lot, whereas now fellas are putting the ball over the bar from their own half-back line.

That time, in the 60s, a fella in the middle of the field would only be able to manage to drop it into the goal area... the ball was slower, heavier and he wasn't able to drive it as far.

Tony Doran struck two goals (and also two points) in his senior championship debut as Wexford totally demolished Laois, 6-10 to 1-6, in the Leinster semi-final the following month.

In the Leinster final, Kilkenny were waiting. And there would be no more goals from Doran in the 1967 championship. He started the provincial decider against Pa Dillon again. As Doran knew too well, there was no stronger full-back, or no prouder customer. Dillon was following in a long and imperious line of Kilkenny 'minders' – Jack Rochford, John Holohan, Peter O'Reilly, Paddy Larkin, Pat 'Diamond' Hayden, Jim 'Link' Walsh, and Cha Whelan were the greatest and most successful of Kilkenny full-backs since the turn of the century. Dillon, who would win three All-

Irelands with Kilkenny in 1967, '69 and '72, recalled in Dermot Kavanagh's excellent book, *Kilkenny No.3* how his career nearly came to a premature end because of Wexford.

'My inter-county career covered two periods, one very brief, the other lasting as long as I could possibly make it,' Dillon stated. 'Shortly after making my debut in the spring of 1960, I played in the Leinster final, which we lost to Wexford. The entire experience was over so quickly that I probably didn't benefit much from it. I rejoined the panel in August 1963, and except for a short break in the spring of 1973, remained a member until after that year's All-Ireland final.'

The Freshford man, a farmer like Doran, but who also combined sales duties with Top Oil, was in no mood to allow his opponent an inch. In that same book recounting the lives and times of Kilkenny's great full-backs Dillon had also offered readers a glimpse of his worst nightmare. 'The one big nagging fear that I did have,' he admitted, 'and the longer my career lasted the more pronounced it became, was of being totally outplayed on some big occasion in Croke Park. The longer the playing career, the more inevitable that such a day is around the corner.'

Dillon was on the go seven years. Doran was in year number one, his first Leinster senior final, and Dillon had only recently seen the damage that the young red-headed Wexford man was capable to unleashing.

Dillon was more than ready that afternoon. And while Doran was held scoreless, at the other end of the field Eddie Keher would tot up an unbeatable total of two goals and five points for himself.

It was not just revenge that Dillon and Pat Henderson directly in front of him had on their minds, but building up their run to the 1967 All-Ireland final, which they would do successfully. They took Wexford out of it, 4-10 to 1-12 and would have just the correct amount of momentum to continue on and lift the Liam MacCarthy Cup two months later by seeing off their magnificent rivals, Tipperary.

Wexford were short three of their regulars – Tom Neville, Michael Collins and Willie Murphy – the day of the 1967 Leinster decider; however for the first 40 minutes of the game it appeared that they were dealing positively with this handicap. Kilkenny captain Jim Treacy had won the toss. But he decided to play into the Canal End. He offered Wexford the Railway goal as their first-half target – and he also offered them the help of having the wind at their backs.

Wexford were 0-8 to 0-4 to the good at half-time.

On the resumption, Treacy's choice seemed to have backfired, as Wexford had their heads down and they also had two points on the scoreboard within eight minutes, to just one reply from Kilkenny. Once again, we leave it to the eloquent Paddy Downey of *The Irish Times* to recall for us what happened next.

'... *Then, in the 39th minute, the challengers struck a blow that in most games would have settled the issue beyond further doubt.*

A long free puck by Dan Quigley, who had moved to centre half-back in the first-half, was blocked out by the Kilkenny defence. The ball ran free to Phil Wilson who made ground up the right wing and from 30 yards he crossed a high lob to the left of the square.

Half a dozen hurleys flashed to meet it, Seamus Whelan, the left corner forward, connected and it sped like a bullet past Ollie Walsh. Wexford's lead now was 1-10 to 0-5 – a formidable gap for lethargic Kilkenny to bridge in the remaining 20 minutes.

The Wexford cheers were still ringing when Ollie Walsh's gigantic puck-out reached Jim Bennett on the 21-yards line. The Kilkenny man caught and swung and, reminiscent of a Billy Murphy-John Quirke feat for Cork in an All-Ireland final 26 years ago, the ball was in the net and the green flag waving.

Ironically for Wexford, it was Whelan's goal that triggered Kilkenny's revival. Claus Dunne followed with a point and in the 44th minute, Eddie Keher drove a 21-yards free through a packed goalmouth to cut Wexford's lead to a tottering two points.

Kilkenny were now in full cry and, having weathered a Wexford raid, another huge Ollie Walsh puck-out reached Jim Lynch, who passed to Dunne and the Mooncoin stylist cracked it for goal number three.

Kilkenny now held the lead for the first time in the game – 3-6 to 1-11. A Paul Lynch free balanced the totals for a minute and then Kilkenny came sweeping back again. Keher pointed a free, and in the 49th minute the same player, loping freely through the widening cracks that were appearing in the Wexford defence, shot the fourth goal with a snappy left-handed stroke that was beautifully calculated to avoid Vinny Staples' attempted hook...'

Sure Pat Henderson at that time would only have been 24... he was tall, gangly... but he was filling out at that stage and he would always have a major presence at centre-back whatever size he was... always, that I can remember... he had it from the beginning. He played wing back on the Kilkenny team for his first year or so, but then he moved into centre-back.

I played on him a good bit. We had a good rivalry, he probably dominated me some days... but I had a few good days on him as well. He was very, very strong under the ball or coming out with the ball... so strong, but tough and fair he was too.

Ted Carroll was a long servant on their team at that time, and Ted had previously played centre-back. He had moved back to corner-back and Pat Henderson had come in at centre-back. All three of their full-back line were knocking around for years... Jim Treacy would have been one of the younger lads... Pa Dillon and Carroll had been there for a long time. Tough men, any of them... any day you played on them.

But sure you'd never come across a full-back line on one of the top teams that was not tough in those days.

I'd have played against John Doyle and Tipperary's famous 'Hells Kitchen' very little... John Doyle, Mick Maher and Kieran Carey... I might have only played a league match or tournament match against John Doyle. I never played against Mick Maher, but I would have played against Kieran Carey a few times after that, because he had moved into full-back.

They were as strong as you could find, but I don't think it was any worse than that... things were exaggerated and a certain amount about the whole 'Hells Kitchen' business and other bits and pieces were added to over time.

They were not that dangerous!

When you played against any of those big named defenders, be it Kilkenny or Tipperary, well... you'd be more aware of who you were up against, and a certain bit in awe.

You knew who you were coming up against... it wasn't just

anybody you were trying to beat to the ball.

They were giants of the game.

John Doyle was a big man... he had a pair of shoulders on him that were twice the width of mine, and that was for starters. He had a fiercesome reputation... and Carey was another big man also. There's no doubt that Doyle was a tough operator, but he could hurl with the best of them too.

Doyle did not take prisoners... but at that time very, very few backs were bothered to take prisoners.

Look at Fan Larkin, for instance... Fan had won an All-Ireland with Kilkenny in '63, then he came back into it at the beginning of the 70s again. Now Fan was a small enough man... I don't know what he would have been, but he was not a big man... but he was as tough as they came. He did not back away from anything.

Any full-back line worth its salt would look to take the man out of it... if they could... it was part of the game.

I know some of our own lads at that time in our defence... if they could get near a Kilkenny man at that time... sure they'd try to kill them.

All defenders were like that in a way.

That was just the way it was... and then you had the rest of the Kilkenny team, most of them majestic hurlers... majestic the full length of the field.

Martin Coogan was an outstanding wing back... a left-handed hurler... very good reader of the game. Pat Lawlor started his career as a half-forward with Kilkenny and moved back to wing back... and was a brilliant defender.

Frank Cummins!

Big man and a powerful hurler. Powerful... powerful... Frank was the mainstay of that Kilkenny team for years on end. To hold down a position in the middle of the field as long as he did... he just had to be something special.

Pat Delaney from Johnstown... he was a another tough man, he did not come into the Kilkenny team I'd say until the second-half of his 20s and he was the sort of the man whom the rest of the forward line revolved around. He was the one making all the plays happen... making room for everyone else... centre-forward... taking the knocks... and a fierce man for driving through the middle.

Liam O'Brien, 'Chunky' as we called him... played mostly at midfield... a stylish hurler I can tell you... the ideal complement to Frank Cummins in the middle of the field.

We'd lost the three lads before playing them in the championship in '67, and the loss of those lads was huge to us... Kilkenny might be able to afford to lose three, but we couldn't... not really. We also lost Willie O'Neill, who came in for one of them. He was injured and had to go off. Our goalkeeper Pat Nolan, it turned out afterwards, had broken a thumb in the first-half, but he played on... all of those things added up and put us under pressure when it came to the second-half.

Aw, sure Jesus, when you think of us losing three men like that... and how much room that probably gave Eddie Keher... who was deadly to begin with, no matter who was marking him.

Keher on the field always stood out a mile... he needed very, very little opportunity to turn any ball into a score. Very accurate from play... and then with deal balls... from 21-yard frees... anything thereabouts, he was always a big goal danger. His reading of the game was amazing... at that time he was the standout forward in the Kilkenny team, and probably the standout forward in the country.

There was no double-teaming a player in those days... you went out and played man to man. That was how it was.

With the likes of Keher... a back might think he had him in his pocket... maybe... but all Eddie Keher needed was one little bit of a slip... and he was gone!

I didn't get a score against them at the other end, not that day. It would have happened at times...

I'd always be disappointed if I didn't get a score, but after a defeat you would be completely down anyway... I didn't really think *about it for too long, whether I scored or didn't score... all that mattered was whether you won or lost.*

That was all that mattered.

Always.

Chapter 3

Tony Doran and Pa Dillon were back at it at the start of 1968. They came face-to-face once again in a league game in Nowlan Park – All-Ireland champs V's National league champs; a heavyweight clash of two teams to whet the appetite of hurling folk all over the country.

Directly in front of the Kilkenny goalkeeper, Ollie Walsh there was a secondary, but no less of a heavyweight contest going on between Dillon and Doran. At half-time Kilkenny led 0-8 to 0-5. They stretched this lead by two points in the third quarter, but just when it looked like it was a day in which both defences would keep a clean sheet, Doran got the better of Dillon.

He deftly eluded the Kilkenny full-back and quickly handballed the sliotar past Walsh. It was a goal that would become a Doran trademark – winning the high ball and making room, and putting the ball away with his hand. Doran scored in the 19th minute of the half, but Wexford's tails did not stay up for very long. Jim Lynch, who had just come into the Kilkenny attack caught the ball from a Paddy Moran centre and gave Pat Nolan in the Wexford goal no chance whatsoever.

Wexford, however, dominated the next 10 minutes and set about more goals in order to get back into the game. None were coming.

Kilkenny held out by 1-10 to 1-7. Wexford had beaten Laois and drawn with Offaly in earlier games in the defence of their league title. Two weeks later they would trounce Tipperary by 11 points in New Ross, and have a goal to spare over Waterford in Dungarvan, but in a play-off game in Croke Park at the end of March they finally relinquished their hold on the same title when Tipp avenged that earlier loss, 1-19 to 5-5.

In the Leinster campaign, Wexford defeated Dublin in the semi-final by 10 points. Tony Doran had a very good day scoring 2-2, but despite having it relatively easy on this occasion Doran always held Dublin, and Laois and Offaly, and other teams who were endeavouring to make their major breakthrough, in the highest regard.

Doran knew how hard it was to make that 'break'.

In addition, he loved playing with lads from the other counties when they were all handed Leinster jerseys, and got the opportunity to size up Munster teams who it appeared had far richer seams to take advantage of through the entire province. There always had been a magic to the Railway Cups, however, ever since as a 15 years-old Tony Doran had taken the train with a few of his friends to see Leinster take on Munster in Croke Park, in both hurling and football.

It was the first time he got to see Christy Ring in full flight.

Des Foley was outstanding... a big strapping fella... before I ever got to play with Wexford I had watched Des playing for Dublin and he was a phenomenal player... unreal, always catching your eye, and when I started to play he was the very same. He was one of the greatest midfielders whoever played the game... I'm talking about the late 50s, 60s... huge man... I actually played with Des in Railway Cups in the late 60s. Maybe his last year or two.... I didn't know him that well, but he was a genuine, very straight fella.

I was fortunate enough to win seven Railway Cups with Leinster... and I was captain in '71, and again in '77, when we beat Munster!

We won five of them in-a-row... I always found playing with

Leinster a huge honour, especially around those years when Wexford and Kilkenny were touch and go with one another, and the majority of the Leinster team bar a couple were made up of Wexford and Kilkenny.

Funny enough we always seemed to gel very well together... and got on very well together playing for the province. The Wexford and Kilkenny players at that time put a lot of work into the Railway Cup and thought it a great thing... especially if we got to beat Munster.

Usually, there was a trial game before the semi-final... the provincial champions against the rest.

It was to get the lads going, I suppose, and to see what we had. Everyone turned out for them, and everyone wanted to play in the Railway Cup.

It was always great to share a dressing-room with those Kilkenny players. We all got on every well together... we always backed one another up.

I suppose... y'know, Munster hurling was always regarded much superior to Leinster and we thought it was a bit of a feather in our cap to get one over on them.

Usually, you'd have a sprinkling of players from Dublin... Offaly, Laois... Des Foley, Mick Bermingham... later on you had Harry Dalton... Pat Quigley would have played also.

Pat was a Tipperary man... played for Dublin at that time... then he went back and played for Tipp... and has now lived in Wexford for a long number of years, being principal in St Peter's College. He played on some of the winning Leinster teams in the 70s. The Offaly fellas were coming through... Padraig Horan in particular would have been featuring, and fellas like Barney Moylan. A regular on the Leinster teams in those years was Pat Dunny from Kildare, a great hurler, outstanding... Pat would have held his own in any county if he got the chance. Mick Mahon from Laois, at wing back, was another outstanding player and then in the late 70s Paddy Quirke from Carlow came to the forefront.

As I say, '71 was a great moment for me... and the fact that Leinster had not beaten Munster in a final for four or five years made it all the greater. We'd go back to the Ashling Hotel after matches, across from Heuston Station... but once the business was done and we had eaten together, we'd all go our separate ways. Business was business... no such thing as a big night out... that was not what it was about.

It was about doing the business against Munster on the field and going home.

It was such a major thing for us.

Cork and Tipp were dominant in those years... the aristocrats of the game. In the 70s, anything to stop a Munster stranglehold was a good thing and winning the Railway Cup helped us... it helped both Kilkenny and Wexford, we felt, anytime we managed to do that.

During that period in the 70s my brother, Colm also played on a lot of those Leinster teams and my Buffers Alley clubmates, Paddy Kavanagh and Mick Butler, also played during that period. It was very special for Buffers Alley to have four Railway Cup medalists during that decade.

It was down to Wexford and Kilkenny again in another Leinster final in 1968. It was always going to be tight. The finest of margins, as it turned out, proved to be the difference – one single point in a seven-goal contest.

At a time when most hurling and football counties throughout the country sought the benefit of a 'brains trust' to scheme and finally craft momentous victories – and groups of selectors on the sidelines sometimes numbered seven and eight men – Wexford in 1968 found themselves winning games because of the gut instinct and brilliant insight of just one man.

Padge Kehoe was Wexford manager, and although he would consult and seek the counsel of other experienced hurling men who were his selectors before and during games, it was becoming evident that he possessed the courage to make the biggest calls himself. In Wexford's 11 points win over Tipperary some months earlier, for example, it was Kehoe who was identified by the men in the press box as the guiding hand in a morale-boosting win.

'Padge Kehoe, Wexford's present team manager, and the architect of many of his county's great victories in his playing days, was the schemer of the Slaneysiders' easy victory over Tipperary in the National Hurling League at New Ross yesterday – a win that maintained Wexford's interest in the destination of the title of which they are holders,' declared one of the press pack, before further explaining himself. *'It was Kehoe's switch after ten minutes which saw full forward Tony Doran and centre forward Jack Berry exchange places, that transformed the Wexford side and ended Tipperary's period of dominance.*

'The visitors, shaping quite well despite facing the wind, had edged into a point lead after 18 minutes when Doran, securing possession 40 yards out, beat several men and passed to the unmarked Berry, who pulled first time and gave John O'Donoghue no chance. Berry, a late minute replacement for Tom Neville in a much reshuffled Wexford team, consolidated his side's position nine minutes later when he fastened onto a centre by Paul Lynch and beat O'Donoghue again...'

Padge was manager... and Ned Power trainer.

They worked well together. Padge from Enniscorthy and Ned from Slieverue in Kilkenny, but teaching in St Peter's College.

Padge could be an abrupt sort of fella, but he was always very straight. Padge had played for so long, 15 or 16 years or more... he was the first manager I could recall in the county. Before that it was five selectors or whatever the number was... he had five selectors as well and they all had a say in the team... and the chairman and secretary as well... maybe eight or nine

I did not know the workings of it at the time, but if it came down to a call between two players then the majority ruled... I reckon.

Padge was a strongly built fella... a fella who had huge respect from his playing days. He'd played till his late 30s and had won three All-Irelands and was highly respected... and he was a fella then who was his own man and did not mind standing on toes. If he had something on his mind then he would come out with it... say it.

I suppose I got on the receiving end from Padge, the same

amount as everyone else... but I also got on well with Padge. If you did something you should not have done he'd let you know. Everyone at different times heard what was not being done right.

Ned, on the other hand, was much quieter, laid back, reserved... he was not your out-going person, but within the group he was not afraid to open up and talk to us as well and as a coach-trainer he was well regarded. Ned was not a tracksuit trainer... Ned would turn out in the same outfit he wore teaching in Peter's that same day... tie, shirt, shoes... his socks pulled up over the bottom of his trousers.

If it was raining, it would not worry Ned in the least. I never saw a cap or hat on him in his life. Whistle around his neck and that was it. And he was involved with Wexford teams throughout the 60s and 70s and never changed.

Padge would get involved a certain amount, but he would leave most of the hard training to Ned. Padge would be in his street clothes too, and the selectors were the same... nobody dressed up for training. Padge was not much of a man for a shirt and tie. He could be wearing a t-shirt and a jacket over it. He did not pussy-foot around about things. He was very straight and everyone knew where they stood with him.

He did not take a fancy to any one player... everyone was treated the same.

For the Leinster final, Kilkenny were without their King of goalkeepers, Ollie Walsh, who was serving a six months suspension. Into his place came a young buck by the name of Noel Skehan who would, soon enough, be talked about in the same gushing conversations as Walsh. On July 15, 1968, Skehan, from the very start, proved his undoubted worth. At half-time in the final Wexford were in front, 1-8 to 1-4.

But it was a game that continued to hold everyone watching breathless. One example was John Teehan and Doran trading goals, one after the other.

Teehan had sent in a long lobbed ball from a sideline and somehow it made its way through a cluster of raised sticks and landed in the Wexford net. Within a minute the ball was on the Kilkenny 50 yards line, and seconds later Doran had it in his grasp and sure enough whipped it to the back of the Kilkenny net.

Both sets of supporters were drowning one another out with their cheering. It was point for point, goal for goal, though crucially it was Skehan who was being asked to save Kilkenny's bacon more often than Pat Nolan at the other end. Skehan had six brilliant saves to his name by the end of the first-half alone.

Teehan's second goal in the second-half might have broken Wexford hearts, especially as he followed it quickly with a point, but Wexford replied with points from Lynch, Jacob and Lynch again. A '70' from Seamus Cleere fell softly to the Wexford net. At the other end, Jack Berry sent an impossibly low shot past Skehan. Then Claus Dunne beat Pat Nolan.

It was a game that demanded nerves of steel, and Wexford had them. It was a game that also demanded goals and while Wexford lost that particular shootout 4-3, a brace of goals from Doran were simply invaluable. Wexford fell over the finish line with a point to spare.

Wexford 3-13, Kilkenny 4-9.

As the countdown to the All-Ireland final commenced, it quickly became apparent that Tipperary were extremely peeved by what they had read about themselves in the national newspapers, and decided to shut up shop when a reporter asked a question or two.

'It is quite impossible to form any firm opinion on the basis of up-to-the-minute information,' wrote one giant in the press box, *'... and trends, because while there has been free access to Wexford's preparations and generous co-operation from Wexford's officials, the opposing camp, through its County Board, has refused to release information to this writer, amongst others.'*

Cork had looked weak enough against Tipp in the Munster final, and while Clare had put up a bigger fight in the semi-final down south, it was still thought that Tipperary would have too much armour, too many heavy guns, for their All-Ireland final opponents. They had also got the better of Kilkenny in the National league final and possessed Wexford's old league title.

However, the members of the press reminded each other, and their readers, that the same advantage appeared to be Tipperary's when the two counties had met in the 1960 All-Ireland final, but that Wexford had confounded all of the forecasters to land their fourth, and last, Liam MacCarthy Cup by 2-15 to 0-11. Though Tipp had taken their revenge in 1962, and again in '65, on the biggest stage.

The members of the press bristled at how they were being treated by Tipperary, but still nodded their heads in Tipp's general direction.

It was a whole new experience as far as I was concerned anyhow... playing in a senior All-Ireland final. We were playing Tipperary, a legendary team... and Tipp were hot favourites going into it.

Everyone fancied them and even though we had beaten Kilkenny in the Leinster final we were not expected to do too much... and that showed in the first-half, I suppose, when they built up their big lead.

We were still in cars heading up to Dublin... we never travelled any other way to Croke Park, only in cars. Wexford were in the senior and minor finals that day, so... we went with Pat Laffan, a local hackney car at the time. He was driving usually the Buffers Alley and Oulart players and he'd normally drive us all as we were side-by-side as parishes... pick us up at our houses.

I was lucky in that way... that I was the last to be picked up normally and the first to be dropped home afterwards. But for that final, there was only Buffers Alley fellas in the car because of the two games. We had a couple of minors and couple of seniors. Pat had one of those big old time cars.

He was a fella who drove slowly... he was never a fast man, and we'd get onto him to hurry up. In that time, if you were doing 50 miles an hour you were driving fast. All the lads would get onto him and tell him to get a heavier sole on his shoe.

Myself and Mick Kinsella, and Tom Donohue from Buffers Alley who was a selector with the seniors... and we had Mick Butler and Martin Casey on the minor team... that was our car load... a big load... we always had a full car.

Five in the car and the driver...

And all the bags of gear, and sticks, of course.

Tony had cleaned his boots the night before. It was only for the big matches, and if he was to run out onto Croke Park, then he'd give them a spit and shine, though on a few occasions he caught his mother taking them up and considering them, before deciding that some action had to be taken.

'Don't do that!' Tony would tell her, '… I'll give them a few bangs… knock the dirt off them!'

But his mother would be intent on having her boy looking his best. And Tony Doran's boots did look more respectable when he played in the 1968 All-Ireland final than they had looked in a long time, because it was the only time his mother ever went to see him play for Wexford.

One match, and one match only.

Tony also had two sticks to his name at the time of his first senior final.

I'd say if I had two I was doing very, very well… I'd say that. I had two at that time to the best of my knowledge.

We always had our own sticks since we were boys.

We'd buy them in various different places… my father always made sure we had a stick… we were never short of one. When he was younger and helping to run the club he'd go to Randalls in Killurin, between Enniscorthy and Wexford, for hurleys for the club. Once or twice a year he'd go down there… and I'd always sit in and go with him. I'd say in fairness, old John Randall, the hurley maker at that time… he'd never see a youngster walking out of his place without handing him a stick.

Other times you'd get them through the school… there were shops in Gorey that sold hurleys… Swords and Morrisseys used to do them… we'd often get them there, or from the club, but we always got them one way or the other

There'd be a clatter of hurling sticks in the house the whole time.

The Randalls were making hurls (not hurleys in their language) for four generations, for teams all over the country, but especially ensuring that hurlers representing Wexford were suitably armed. Bobby Rackard was a

Randall's man, as were legendary stickmen like Liam Dunne and Martin Storey. The Randalls produced true Wexford hurls – hurls with thicker heads, more designed for ground hurling. John Randall would only use the bottom three feet of the ash tree for his hurls, getting 12 or 13 sticks from each tree. And, importantly, a foot of the ash coming from the tree below the ground before it meets its root system, and making a perfect turn on the hurl.

Tony Doran had two Randall hurls in the boot of Pat Laffan's old car, though neither had the name of T Doran spelled midway down the stick.

I didn't worry too much about what stick I had to start a match with. If you had a hurl for a while and you were playing well you might like it, but ...

At that time, bands were around hurls all the time... they were broken and mended again. The tape we put on the hurls was black insulating tape... that was it, no such thing as specialised tape. Nowadays they have different types of tape... and toweling-type tape ... but we just used rolls of black insulating tape if we were putting anything on the handles. That was it... but it would stick to your hands, and you'd have very black hands at the end of the game.

I'd be preparing it for big matches, small matches, anything... I'd look after it all the time. I never had my name on a stick. Not like now... you see fellas going to club matches even now and they have three or four hurls... y'know, and they'd have them marked down with their name and number... 1, 2, 3 and 4.

Most fellas would be like that now.

I didn't prepare for the All-Ireland final any differently than I had prepared for any other match that year... don't believe I did. And I slept great the night before the game. I never had a problem sleeping before a match or anything like that. You would have a certain amount of nerves... but I can't recall anything out of the ordinary regarding '68. We carried on as normal.

You would suffer a certain amount of nerves any time you were heading up to Croke Park, but they would never get the better of you. I remember in the build up, the media spotlight was all on us at the time as there was a media ban in Tipperary.

They were unhappy with the Independent and Irish Press... the two main papers... I think that they had fallen out with them over what was said about their league final win against Kilkenny. They felt they got bad press and they put the ban on.

That left the media with just us to deal with.

Two weeks before the All-Ireland final, Tony Doran received his first visit from one of the 'giants' of the national press. John D Hickey, in his best suit, wearing his spectacles and looking sort of regal, but certainly assuming the role of a legendary and widely read figure, called into the Doran house looking for their boy who was playing in the All-Ireland final.

Hickey didn't call beforehand.

The giants of newspapermen did not ask for interviews. They would arrive, or descend if you like, and there was no question of them not being entertained by whomever they had decided to interview. No more than a Bishop or a TD would be told that they didn't pick the best day to drop in!

A photographer was with John D Hickey.

And Hickey, a Tipperary man, who would suffer occasional accusations that Tipp blood flowed more steadily through his veins than any other, received a generous welcome. Though Tony was not in the house.

He was out in one of the fields.

Hickey set out to find Tony, and his photographer would grab a shot of Tony before too long, sitting up on his tractor midway through his day's work, but with a smile on his face. The photograph appeared across four columns, sitting on top of Hickey's article in *The Irish Independent* the following week.

Oh yeah... it was a big deal, and something out of the ordinary. John D never made an appointment or anything... he just turned up. He got directions... at the time we had a farm in Ballygarrett which was seven or eight miles away from the home house.

We were bringing in bales of hay and packing them away in a shed the day he arrived. Small bales and packing away we were, when he showed up out of the blue... some of the brothers were with me. Next thing... John D Hickey shows up in the yard, and he marches up to me.

That was my first experience of a journalist... meeting one face-to-face. In his suit and all business, he was... everyone wore suits when they were doing anything important then. We chatted for half an hour... or an hour, the two of us just standing there in the shed.

It was a fine summer's day... my first big interview. You had only ever heard about these fellas with their famous names... we'd seen their names in the papers all of our lives... we would have read everything they had written about games for years.

There was nobody else to read... there was only a couple of papers in the country.

There was John D Hickey in the Independent ... Padraig Puirseal in the Irish Press... just the few of them... Mick Dunne... Paddy Downey in the Times... Donal Carroll in the Independent years later after John D... that was about it. They were the men who told everyone what was happening and who was playing well.

The Doran family also owned a milk lorry at the time.

Cans of milk were collected from local farms and brought to the creamery in Ballycanew. The milk round covered approximately 15 miles … and cans were normally 10 gallons in size, so when full there was quite a lot of manual work involved.

Joe Doran had made the round with a tractor and trailer to begin with in the mid 60s, but they graduated to a lorry fairly quickly. But in summertime when the milk was more plentiful, it was sometimes necessary to build a deck on the lorry so that extra cans could be taken. It slowed up the whole operation, and mornings with an extra deck meant more chatting with neighbours, which was fine normally, but on the week of an All-Ireland final there could be too much talk about the match.

Everyone only wished him the best, but there was only so much time Tony could give to thinking about the biggest match of his young life.

There were up to 25 farms to be visited… and he liked to be in Ballycanew most mornings by ten o'clock.

Some of the other lads would usually start off the collection and I would take over when the lorry was passing by our home place and complete the collecting, and then travel to the creamery. On arrival you'd have to wait your turn to be unloaded… for the cans to be taken off, left on the platform and then emptied into a scales for weighing.

Everyone's individual cans… then get them back into the lorry. It'd be early to mid-afternoon before it would be all done, and the same every day… seven days a week. That was one of my main jobs… yeah… as I was usually the one who did the milking at home.

But everyone was talking about the match… and a few days before I stayed off the lorry to avoid the talking… but I was back with the cans and doing the round on the Tuesday morning after the All-Ireland.

A generation ago, there was no question of players meeting up the night before an All-Ireland final. The Wexford team to meet Tipperary had been picked the previous Sunday, and the final night of training had been the Tuesday.

Our dressing-room before the game… it was a bit hectic.

It was fairly rushed because we had Wexford in the minor final, and we all stayed out and watched the minors till their game was over. We all stayed out there… still in our street-clothes… what else would we be wearing? We were all out there sitting on the grass… in front of the wall of the Cusack Stand.

I've seen lots of photographs of the whole line of us all sitting there sitting on the grass. The crowd behind us… and we stayed till the very end, because it was a tight match and nobody told us to go in… the lads were playing Cork and they won it by three points in the end.

So we stayed out there.

By the time we got back into the dressing-room and got togged out there was no time to do much. There was no time to get worried about our game or anything like that... it was all a bit of a rush.

It had also been a long, long wait.

Most of the cars bringing the players to Croke Park contained the minor and senior players.

Pat Laffan pulled into the ground a good hour before the minor game was due to begin… and almost two and a half hours before the senior match was due to get underway.

There was no food for the senior lads either. No quick snacks, no energy drinks, nothing at all to help them to refuel as they were sitting on the grass in the heat of a ground that was fast filling up with spectators, but which would finish with an attendance that was 10,000 less than the number who watched Wexford upset Tipperary in the 1960 final. Eight years later there were 63,461 in Croke Park, most of them thinking Tipp would do it.

There was no food in the dressing-room.

In Croke Park all there ever was was a cup of tea at half-time... tea with lots of sugar in it. When you think about it now and think about lads fuelling themselves up now before games and eating all of the right things!

None of that back then... if you wanted something you'd have to run to the back of the Cusack Stand and buy something off one of the women selling bars of chocolates from their prams.

We were sitting there all that time... out there at the foot of the Cusack. It was a fine day... there was no team suits... we were wearing whatever suits we all had at home.

At the time that was it... there was no question of a team getting a tailor to fit everyone into the same style of a suit... God no!

My big memory is that there wasn't an awful lot of time to pussy-foot around before the game once we got back into that dressing-room.

It should have been no great surprise to anybody, therefore, that Wexford failed to get out of the starting blocks in a hurry once the ball was tossed in.

Throughout the field, from the very start, Tipperary were completely dominating. I started on Mick Roche... he was outplaying me in every way... every way possible.

Type of player he was, Mick was covering in behind all the rest of the backs as well... he seemed to be in the right position to claim every single ball that came in.

In that same period I got a couple of chances... didn't take them. No matter where he went, the ball went in his direction... he was completely dominating the line.

He was a big man, and a very athletic type of fella.

Mick was also a fella with a big, black curly head of hair on him... and this might come as a surprise to some people, but he used to wear a hair net over his head to control the hair.

No helmets at that time... no, none.

I felt good at that time... I didn't feel phased by the occasion or the parade, or anything... but when the game started it was a different story... and we were all at sixes and sevens...

I never wore a helmet in my whole career... I don't know why? I did not try really hard to wear one... I put on one a couple of times and it didn't feel comfortable... never bothered about it after that. Donal Clifford of Cork, I think, was the first player to wear a helmet... I can't remember anyone from Wexford wearing one till well into the 70s.

Mick Roche wore the net to keep the hair down... and before the match started he put the net out in front of his chest and asked me to hold the corner of the net as he spread it out.

Strange thing to ask of an opponent when you think of it? I was standing beside him minding my own business, I suppose. Then he piped up, and I looked around at him.

'Hold the corner of the net there!' he told me, '... while I spread it out.'

It surprised me.

But I did what he asked me.

It was the only time I was ever asked to do anything like that on a hurling field. The net would stay on Mick's head, and keep the hair flattened down. I never saw anyone else do it.

All of this happened before the national anthem.

And they were the only words we had to say to one another.

The first-half of the 1968 All-Ireland final proceeded to go by in a flash. When the teams returned to their dressing-rooms for their tea Tipperary were leading 1-11 to 1-3. Tipperary had been 0-8 to 0-1 in front after 20 minutes, and a fifth All-Ireland title in a joyous decade looked imminent for the Premier County. Mick Roche was indeed looking majestic. Next to him Len Gaynor was unbeatable. After 24 minutes, a Donie Nealon lineball got a touch from Jimmy Doyle to the net. It was 1-9 to 0-3. Another score made it a 10-point advantage before, out of nothing, Jack Berry sneaked a goal back for Wexford.

'We were very fortunate to be only eight points behind at half-time!' goalkeeper, Pat Nolan would tell reporters afterwards. Vinny Staples was in agreement. 'I did not think we had a chance of winning at half-time, but by the time Padge Kehoe was finished talking to us...'

Kehoe's words at half-time in the Wexford dressing-room would become legendary. Whether he actually spoke for a long, or a short period of time, remains uncertain. Accounts from different players have varied.

But, certainly, Kehoe said enough.

In the week before the match, the Wexford manager had told Paddy Downey of *The Irish Times* that he had no doubt, whatever happened or befell Wexford, that his team would win the All-Ireland. 'Wexford have the will to win... and they will win,' he asserted. 'The team has trained better than any I've seen since 1960, and a great deal of credit for that goes to our trainer, Ned Power who has done a wonderful job with the minors as well as the seniors.'

Kehoe had played in six All-Ireland finals himself, winning three, and losing as many, and had enjoyed ruling the country alongside Nickey Rackard and Co in 1955 and '56. He would indeed talk his players into turning around the 1968 All-Ireland final and defying all the odds in the second-half. He would see Wexford land their sixth All-Ireland title, when the county was in Liam Griffin's hands, in 1996 but despite winning it all, in football and hurling in his native county, and earning as many friends in racing and coursing circles, in addition to breeding winners for the greyhound track in Enniscorthy, Padge Kehoe would ask before passing 11 years later that his funeral be a quiet affair, with no guard of honour.

The crowds still descended on Enniscorthy to say their good-byes to Padge Kehoe, and they came from all over the country, and all over Wexford, to find his coffin draped with the Wexford and St Adian's GAA jerseys.

At half-time we didn't think it was gone... in the last five or 10 minutes of the half we had been getting back into the game a little bit... we should have got a few more scores. I personally was one of these fellas who always thought we had a chance... I always thought we would win matches.

I had a word with Christy Jacob as we came back onto the field... I said to him that if we got a quick score we'd be right back in the game.

One fairly early.

Padge had laid into us a certain amount.

I can't recall what he had said... I'd read some of the reports about what he had said and what he had done, and I think they were exaggerated a little bit. But he would have given the table a few thumps with the hurl alright.

No doubt about it... there were cups of tea on the table that came into harm's way alright.

He just laid it on the line for us.

Everything he said, he said pretty strongly... but not to any one individual... he told the whole lot of us what he thought of our first-half performance.

Wexford got the first score Tony Doran wanted.

And then Tony Doran scored, possibly, just possibly, the most important goal in his long and amazing career.

We got that first score... Jack Berry got a point and then five minutes later or so I got through.

I had switched to full-forward before half-time... about 10 minutes before the end of the half, and went in on Noel O'Gorman... strong fella, one of the younger fellas on the Tipp team, but a fine young hurler. He had only come onto the Tipp team in the last year or so before the '68 final. Halfway through the second-half he swapped places with John Costigan in the corner... in between my two goals.

It didn't seem we were back on the field very long at all before the ball came in from out the field... and I caught it around the 14- and 21-yard lines... and turned to go to my right, which I nearly always did. Then I switched and struck it on my left... and it was in the corner of the net.

The goalie hardly saw it.

That brought us back into it. Four points in it, and we got another point shortly after that.

Tipp got a score. But Jimmy O'Brien answered it straight away with a point. We missed a few good scores in between. Our half-back line and midfield were dominating the play at that stage. Dan Quigley was controlling the game... if Mick Roche had done it in the first-half, Dan had done it in the second-half. He had played well all through however, but he really pushed it on after that. The full-back line of Tom Neville, Eddie Kelly and Ned Colfer made sure the Tipp inside forwards were kept quiet, and behind them Pat Nolan was superb in our goal.

Dan and Willie Murphy were playing well... Willie had come to terms with Babs Keating in the first-half... Willie was one of these swash-buckling type of players, and Vinny Staples was doing well on the other wing. Phil Wilson and Dave Bernie were lording it in the middle of the field, so there was a steady supply coming to the forwards all the time. In the first-half we had got good ball too but we had not taken our chances.

John O'Donoghue in the Tipp goal made some great saves in the second-half as well to keep us out. Eventually, I got pulled down going through halfway through the second-half... Paul Lynch buried it in the net and that brought us level.

Level game... then they came back at us and it was see-saw hurling, one side to the other... and I got in for a goal with seven or eight minutes left and that put us in front... caught a high ball around the 14 or thereabouts and got inside John Costigan and palmed it into the net... and was nearly looking John O'Donoghue in the eyes when I put it past him.

I scored a good few with my hand when you were allowed to score a goal like that, and usually got close to the 'keepers.

And Jack Berry got another goal shortly after... we got a couple of points, and we were eight up. Tipp came back and got a couple of goals at the end.

We had missed good goal chances and I think we had a goal disallowed in the first-half... and one brought back for a free in the second-half. Even though Tipperary were the better team in the first-half we could have been much closer to them. The goals we got, we got out of nothing, but we should have got better goals.

Paul Lynch went centre-forward and he had cancelled out Mick Roche to a certain extent. Lynch was an artist on the overhead strike and the first time strike, and Roche was still covering deep... and Lynch was there moving good ball to us inside. That made a big difference in the second-half. It helped to take Mick Roche out of the game... any ball he did get he was getting near his own full-back line and was not getting it in an attacking half-back position.

Alongside Lynch, on the wings, John Quigley who had replaced the injured Seamus 'Shanks' Whelan at half-time and Christy Jacob were causing Tipp some trouble with their direct play. Inside, in the corners, Jimmy O'Brien was a real livewire and Jack Berry *was strong and a brilliant opportunist.*

But it was still hard to believe how the game had turned around!

We gave away two goals... they got one from a free... and those two goals in the last minute came about because we had slacked off a certain amount. The first was from Sean McLoughlin, and from a free Babs got their second.

There was no clock over the Canal End back then... you were waiting for the final whistle and thinking how long was left in the match... eight points up we thought it was done and dusted.

When the clock did go up at the Canal End, years later, it was no use to us anyhow because you could never work out how much time exactly was left. You'd still be guessing.

We were glad to hear that whistle from John Dowling. Anything could have happened after their two goals.

Mick Dunne who would later become a household face on RTE was, in 1968, one of the giants in the press box in Croke Park, working for *The Irish Press* newspaper. He saw Wexford's victory over Tipperary thus:

'Wexford 5-8, Tipperary 3-12

Not even the gale swept day in 1956, when another generation of purple and gold hurling heroes snatched the National league from the canyons of defeat, could compare with the astonishingly dramatic victory that Wexford indelibly etched into the annals of the championship at Croke Park yesterday. With a truly astounding recovery, they thundered to another memorable win over Tipperary for their county's fifth All-Ireland senior hurling title.

It was a day of history for Wexford on which they recorded the senior-minor double on their first dual appearance on All-Ireland final day. But, most important of all for the game of hurling itself, this Wexford senior success, after being eight points behind at the interval, was achieved in a second-half of notable hurling splendour, nerve-wracking tension and excitement – and impeccable sportsmanship.

Forget the first half: it matters not at all. Remember only the second half brimful of hurling riches which deserve to be cherished fondly as long as memories remain active. It was a contest waged with healthy hurling ferocity that was commendably devoid of hostility.

Twelve years ago an earlier Wexford team stepped out for the second half against Tipperary 15 points behind, but had the assistance of a storm to aid them on their way to victory. Yesterday, the present-day wearers of the purple and gold, had no strong wind but they did possess intractable resolve, hitherto unrevealed quantities of stamina and a high degree of fitness as well as a latent hurling power and skill.

In that remarkable second-half, a combination of all of these made them All-Ireland champions.

At half-time none even amongst Wexford's most ardent and optimistic supporters, could have given a farthing for their chances. Tipperary ran up a 10 points lead in 26 minutes of playing into the Railway End goal against the slight breeze, and Wexford were being over-powered and over-run.

The Munster champions led 1-11 to 1-3 at half-time and they had performed with such effortlessness and, it seemed, conservation of energy that they appeared to be only at half-pace throughout that one-sided first half. A huge humiliating defeat appeared imminent for Wexford.

But, if magic was ever compounded in a dressing room it must have been concocted in Wexford's yesterday. Perhaps the magician was team manager Padge Kehoe, the one-time star, who pounded the dressing room table during a thunderous lecture to his charges at the interval.

It did the trick. But it was not the only one in Wexford's magic box. For the resumption of the game in which there was a bewildering series of positional switches, Wexford altered their line-up by sending in John Quigley to right corner-forward (later he moved to right half), moving Paul Lynch to the 40 and instructing Tony Doran to camp at the parallelagram after switching to full-forward late in the first half.

It all worked like a charm. Wexford's spirit was renewed and refreshed: there was grit and bold adventure in their second half hurling and they were soon storming back in the chase of Tipperary.

A new wave of resolve swept through the team. The full back line, which had been troubled in the first-half by Lian Devaney and then Michael Keating tightened up very considerably. The half-back line in which Dan Quigley was performing with immense stubbornness, was welded into a unit of new strength by the great improvement in Willie Murphy's play.

Phil Wilson became completely dominant at midfield and as Dave Bernie came into prominence more and more in the second half, Wexford took over control hereabouts;

a dominance that was contributed to by the roaming outfield of, first, Jimmy O'Brien and, later, dynamic John Quigley, and the tremendous support that came from Paul Lynch, who frequently lay back from the '40'.

In addition, the presence of Tony Doran at full-forward caused distress and alarm among the Tipperary full-back line, which never showed the unyielding obduracy of the Doyle-Maher-Carey era. The ball was now frequently driven in chest-high to Doran and the red-headed forward grasped it so securely so often that he caused panic in the Tipp defence. After seven minutes of the second-half John Costigan was switched to full-back from the right corner.

But it did not prevent Doran from causing Tipp's ambitions to crumble. He managed two goals himself. He set up another for Christy Jacob but the whistle had already sounded for a foul on Doran and he presented Jack Berry with a gift chance which was foiled only by splendid anticipation by goalkeeper John O'Donoghue, who dived headlong to a palmed attempt by Berry.

Moreover, it was when Doran was fouled when menacingly in possession in the 46th minute, that Wexford were awarded the free from which Paul Lynch struck the equalising goal.

After that goal there was no stopping Wexford. With the scent of victory in their nostrils, and with an abundance of stamina and speed, they hurled with daredevil arrogance. But, for eight minutes, there was spine-tingling suspense as both sides strove for the score that could break the deadlock.

Keating was wide for Tipperary, O'Donoghue saved from John Quigley and Jack Berry, Doran had a Wexford wide and Keating was astray with a shot at the other end. Then Phil Wilson gained possession at midfield and Paul Lynch flipped the ball further on with an overhead stroke. Doran grabbed it, but despite being harried and bustled, he turned to get a left handed shot past goalkeeper O'Donoghue for a three point lead that was quickly stretched to eight.

Belatedly, Sean McLoughlin and Michael Keating had Tipperary goals, but Wexford were now so exuberantly superior that these could not prevent Tipperary suffering a second successive defeat in the final.

Wexford were so much the masters in the second-half that they were able to win this final with two points to spare even in spite of having two goals annulled because referee John Dowling had blown for frees before the scores were made. The first was in the seventh minute when Jack Berry hand-passed the ball to the net and the second was *in the 34th minute when Jacob had got the ball into the net.*

It took immense courage, therefore, for Wexford to take the title. But they had it in their plenty, from superb goalkeeper Pat Nolan right down through the team. Each member of the side played heroically but none contributed more to this than goalkeeper Nolan, full-back Eddie Kelly, right full-back Tom Neville, half-backs Dan Quigley and, in the second-half, Willie Murphy, midfielder Wilson and forwards Tony Doran, Paul Lynch and Jack Berry – and young John Quigley, who showed steeled indestructibility in his determination when introduced into the attack.

On a day of wonderful goalkeeping John O'Donoghue prevented Wexford from having a bigger victory. Michael Roche was a commanding figure at centre half-back in the first-half, but he was frequently upset by Paul Lynch after the interval. PJ Ryan tried unceasingly at midfield and, in the attack, Michael Keating was the most prominent forward and for half an hour looked as though he would have a field day in scoring. Len Gaynor was also good in defence.

It was a game played in a commendable sporting spirit, as a total of only 20 frees indicates. Referee John Dowling, whose authority was never in doubt, without being imperiously posed, contributed more than a small share to the enjoyment of the occasion.

__Wexford__ – P Nolan; T Neville, E Kelly, E Colfer; V Staples, D Quigley (capt), W Murphy; P Wilson, D Bernie; P Lynch, A Doran, C Jacob; J O'Brien, J Berry, S Whelan. Sub –J Quigley for Whelan.

__Tipperary__ – J O'Donoghue; J Costigan, N O'Gorman, J Gleeson; M Burns, M Roche (capt), L Gaynor; PJ Ryan, D Nealon; M Keating, J Ryan, J Doyle; L Devaney, J McKenna, S McLoughlin. Sub – F Loughnane for Doyle.'

The Wexford dressing-room was like an open house after the game, and all ready for the party of a lifetime.

Nobody was turned away.

All hell broke loose... seemed like an age before we got to the Hogan Stand to get the cup and all. The fact of having come back like we did had everyone excited.

The dressing-room was open door to anyone to come in... journalists, anyone... they were all in there... never any closed door in Croke Park back then.

We had our meal back in Bray, in the hotel and I suppose fellas were drinking... and were on the beer for the night, and those of us who weren't drinking were sitting there looking at them... and that was about the size of it.

There were a good few non-drinkers on the Wexford team. Very few heavy drinkers either... half the team didn't drink, I'd say.

There was that night in Bray and then home... the reception in Wexford... we went through all the main towns... Gorey and Ennsicorthy... we didn't go to New Ross till the following Sunday.

It was 12 o'clock before we hit Wexford town and got something to eat in the Talbot Hotel. We all came back home in our same cars we had travelled up to Dublin in the day before... the whole way... driving together... crawling through the crowds.

Early Tuesday morning when I got home!

I didn't talk to my mother and father till much later on that Tuesday morning.... didn't see them on the field... or outside the ground after the match.

I did not get to see them or talk to them in Bray either ... and they were both asleep in bed when I got home in the early hours on the Tuesday morning.

There were no mobile phones back then... you had no contact with people unless you bumped into them. I was dropped home by Pat Laffin, and I went straight to bed.

There was nobody up in the house.

And it was back to things as normal the next day... collecting the milk cans in the truck and heading to the creamery in Ballycanew.

I'm pretty sure it was on the Tuesday morning that I was back to work.

Chapter 4

When the newly crowned All-Ireland champions ran out in front of their own, and received a guard of honour onto the field in Gorey from Offaly on October 27 – just over a month since humbling mighty Tipperary – nobody was to guess that the same company they were keeping that afternoon would terminate their ambitions of retaining their title. It was the opening game of a whole new season, and Offaly were visitors for the first round of the National league.

Though Offaly did not bend the knee once the whistle sounded, and only lost out on a full scoreboard by 6-14 to 5-8.

There were 11 goals that afternoon, another afternoon of maximum excitement, but significantly Offaly had learned how to slice through the defence of the greatest team in the country. They did not forget!

In the early summer of 1969, they would score another five goals and thereby force Wexford to make an early and quite shocking exit from the Leinster Championship. But that was down the road…

Wexford were to enjoy a long and almost successful league campaign.

When the league resumed after only one game pre-Christmas, Wexford had two points to spare over Kilkenny in Wexford Park (2-6 to 2-4), and there followed a brilliant one-point victory over Tipperary in Thurles (3-12 to 2-14). Seven goals were crashed home against Waterford in New Ross. One week later, in Portlaoise, 11 goals were recorded against Laois, though in the semi-final of the league in Nowlan Park sense was restored on the scoreboard – and defences ruled – as Wexford forced themselves past Limerick by 2-5 to 1-6.

Wexford had the chance to add a league title to their All-Ireland crown when they met Cork in the final of the competition in Croke Park on May 4.

But, we need to reverse up!

And go back to February 10, when Wexford managed to once more put Kilkenny to the sword by two points. It was a win that was founded on the expert awareness and skills of Pat Nolan in the Wexford goalmouth.

Nolan had saved them that afternoon when the Cats were frantic at the end for a match-winning goal. Wexford had led 1-4 to 0-3 at the end of a quiet enough first-half, and they still had five points in hand with less than a minute remaining when Kilkenny were awarded a 21-yards free and Eddie Keher hurtled the sliotar to the back of the net.

Their tails were up and Kilkenny had two more goal chances in front of the crowd of 4,000. Both were thwarted by Nolan, expertly, confidently, supremely; the last save showing breathtaking reflexes as he stopped a crashing drive from the visiting centre-forward, Pat Delaney. It was an afternoon when Pa Dillon held Tony Doran scoreless at the other end of the field. Nolan's performance, therefore, was doubly important.

Kilkenny had two of the greatest goalkeepers in the country in Ollie Walsh and Noel Skehan, but, in truth, the greatest counties in the game relied on expert net minders, Wexford included.

Tony Doran had a front row view of Walsh and Skehan.

I'm not sure how much of a pleasure it was… to be able to see the two of them up close. They were incredible… magnificent.

In all my years playing with Wexford I only ever faced two Kilkenny goalkeepers… Walsh or Skehan… y'know! Ollie was there for a good few years before I started. Skehan came in then and was there for a long time and finished up the same year as myself.

Very hard to compare them, because you are comparing different eras as well... in Ollie Walsh's time the goalkeeper was fair game for opposing forwards and all, and in Noel Skehan's era the goalie was very different... the goalie could not be tackled at that stage. It was very hard to separate the two of them... Ollie was more of a... what could I call him?

Flamboyant... that type of character?

He loved to get possession, take on three or four forwards and get well away from his goal before he left the ball up the other end of the field. He liked doing that.

As a shot stopper he was also outstanding.

Noel Skehan?

Noel was not like Ollie in that way. He was someone who played on his goal-line... but the thing about Noel Skehan was... he had a great eye. He could make great saves. Outstanding... the two of them were simply outstanding and they covered something like 30 years in goal for Kilkenny.

Pat, for us, was a fantastic keeper also... what can I say about Pat? For a start, he is a relation of mine, but Pat was maybe a different type of a goalie again from Walsh and Skehan.

He was more laid back and quieter as a character, but he was an outstanding man at stopping shots and he put in the best part of 20 years service to Wexford... at a time when Wexford were at or near the top all of the time.

He would have gone about his job in a quieter way.

Wexford were afraid of nobody at the beginning of 1969. Why should they doubt themselves? Even though the league final did put a hole in the thought that the team might be bulletproof in their All-Ireland title defence.

Then, of course, there were those goals conceded against Offaly earlier in the league campaign.

We were scoring lots of goals and we were moving reasonably well...

we had those big wins over Waterford and Laois... we were going very well alright.

And even when we lost to Cork in the league final, we still felt that we were in good order. Wexford and Cork had a long history... famous days. In the 50s, Wexford and Cork had huge respect for one another... Ring, Rackard, O'Donnell... I suppose the Wexford team of that period were known as great sportsmen... big men, but they had a reputation for being a fair team and that came through against Cork on the biggest day of all. When you think about it now, all of these years later, it is hard to believe alright... Wexfordmen lifting an opponent off the field, but that's what they did.

Ring was going for a record ninth All-Ireland at the time, and it was the first time Wexford had beaten one of the top two teams... in an All-Ireland final, and it was just something that happened.

Wexford players actually put Christy Ring up on their shoulders after the game... different time, incredible... but it shows you what kind of men they were back then... the fellas who played for Wexford and for Cork in those days.

When Wexford and Cork had met in the All-Ireland final in 1954, in front of a record crowd of 84,856, the game was dominated by two central figures. Ring would win a record eighth All-Ireland medal for himself, but Bobby Rackard would give a classical display of defensive hurling that was not equalled for several decades when he moved from centre-half to full-back in the second period of the game after Nick O'Donnell's collar-bone was broken by a ball struck from close range by the Cork maestro. Cork won 1-9 to 1-6.

Two years later, the defining moment of the final between the same two teams came when Ring went for the winner, and Wexford goalkeeper Art Foley not only stopped the sliotar, but he held it in his hand and cleared the ball back up the field. It turned the tide for Wexford who won the game 2-14 to 2-8.

At the end of that game came the moment of all moments, when Bobby Rackard and Nick O'Donnell carried Ring off the field on their shoulders.

All three of them… giants!

In the 1969 National league final, Tony Doran had the great honour of leading out the Wexford team against one of their greatest of foes.

It was described, in parts, by Paddy Downey in the pages of *The Irish Times* thus:

'Cork hurling shone with much of its old glitter in Croke Park yesterday, when the most accomplished team to wear the famed red jerseys since 1956 beat the All-Ireland champions Wexford in a thrilling National Hurling League final. But that glitter did not really appear until the second-half, and then only from the eight minute onwards, when two goals in less than sixty seconds set the Munster side on the road to their first League title since 1953 and their seventh in all since the competition began in 1926.

To Wexford as much as to Cork must go the thanks of the 31,963 spectators for a very fine game. True, there were phases in the first-half that were less than satisfying to the neutral connoisseur: phases when the stickwork of a number of players on both sides was neither fully fluent nor fully proficient and when traces of rancour influenced the tough exchanges around both goalmouths.

Before the merits of a notable Cork victory are analysed, the story of Wexford's misfortunes must be told. First of all, they were forced to line out without their regular full back, Eddie Kelly, who was injured in the semi-final against Limerick. Then, after only two and a half minutes of play, they lost their great centre half-back, Dan Quigley, who broke a finger in a clash with the Cork centre-forward, and saw their full-forward, Seamus Whelan depart with an injured ankle six minutes before half time.'

Still, Wexford looked good for their win.

Until the Cork selectors decided to switch things around in the 36th minute of the game! Wexford had led 0-6 to 0-5 at the interval, and playing into the Railway end in the second-half they added another point. Then Cork switched Willie Walsh and Charlie Cullinane between the '40'and full-forward.

In the 38th minute a high lob from right half-back, Donal Clifford landed outside the Wexford square and Cullinane raced in and whipped it to the back of the net. Less than a minute later, Charlie McCarthy lost possession when moving through the centre and the ball dribbled out to his right. Walsh, however, followed up smartly and gave Pat Nolan no chance whatsoever.

It finished Cork 3-12, Wexford 1-14.

At the time we still believed we would be there or thereabouts to win the Leinster... and the All-Ireland, y'know? Okay we had lost the league final to Cork, lost by four points in a good game... lost a couple of players again through injury before the Leinster semi-final against Offaly. Maybe we underestimated Offaly a small bit in the run up to it... but we should not have done so, because it was obvious for three or four years against us in league games that they were coming... and they were only a small bit away from the breakthrough.

In '68 they had run Kilkenny to four points in a Leinster semi-final, but we were confident... and we should not have been over confident. Offaly were becoming a force at that stage and they had us beaten in that semi-final before we knew where we were.

Five goals in the first half... they started off flying!

After losing the league final to Cork there were no great alarm bells ringing in our dressing-room. It had been a tight game, a close game... we probably still thought we were reasonably well on course for another All-Ireland... we had lost Dan Quigley in the first few minutes through injury, and he was still missing come championship time.

The two goals from Cork put them in the driving seat.

Dan was a massive player... massive... and the year before in winning the All-Ireland he was the vital man all through the season... from centre-back! I knew what it was like playing against him... I'd come up against him playing for Rathnure quite often.

Dan was an incredible player on any team.

He was a blow to us.

June 30, 1969, was supposed to be a day when Wexford, as defending Leinster and All-Ireland champs, would issue a statement to everyone else thinking of putting as much as a finger on the Liam MacCarthy Cup.

Instead, it was the day when Offaly cut through the Wexford defence and, as they did on the first day of the 1968-69 season, on October 27, helped themselves to five goals. As raiding larders go, it was flamboyant in its execution.

But, twice, Offaly had totted up five goals against the No.1 team in the country. Wexford had survived the first time!

The second time, with all five goals coming in the first-half, there was really no way back. Six minutes in, Paddy Molloy punished a blunder in the Wexford defence to make it 2-1 to 0-0, and it did not get any better. Offaly led by 14 points when the two teams headed back to their respective dressing-rooms, 5-4 to 0-5.

Offaly's first-time pulling had been crisp and accurate. They displayed no hint of an inferiority complex, no fear whatsoever. Ned Buggy, who had come in for Dan Quigley in the League final against Cork, and who had performed hero-like as he filled the Rathnure man's empty boots, did not have one of his better days and was replaced by Padge Kehoe during the interval. Joe Foley was moved back from the attack.

And Wexford did catch their breath. They did score three goals of their own in the second-half. They might have scored more if not for the dynamic display by Damien Martin in the Offaly goals. It ended 5-10 to 3-11.

A five points defeat only, but with the All-Ireland champions left in a heap in Croke Park and facing a long journey home that was so vastly different than their route back south the previous September.

I wouldn't like to take anything away from Offaly's display that day, but they did catch us on the hop. We were not prepared for their quick fire start... we didn't see it coming.

I think Offaly went on to prove themselves in the Leinster final against Kilkenny, and only lost by a point. Kilkenny scored three goals and Offaly scored no goal... they should have kept some of the goals against us from the semi-final and brought them with them. They could have won their first Leinster final very easily that year.

At half-time against them we were in a certain amount of shock... we were not just behind, we were so far behind... and we'd been completely out-hurled into the bargain.

It was not a very nice place to be.

I think everyone was in a state of shock... I can't recall what Padge Kehoe said. We talked about turning it around... but a 14-point lead was massive for them. Five points in the forwards was a fairly meagre score for us to have clocked up.

Chapter 5

The summer of 1970 was only half through when Tony Doran had two more goals behind his name at the end of another long afternoon in Croke Park. He had come up against Pa Dillon once more, in the Leinster final. Doran didn't get any points, just the two goals.

But the two goals meant that in his last 11 championship matches for the Wexford senior hurling team Tony Doran had plundered for a brace of goals an incredible nine times.

It was a strike rate that was indeed astonishing, even at a time when goals were more of a regular currency between the greatest of teams.

He was also getting his fair share in the league as well, of course.

Though the league campaign through the winter and spring was only so-so. Wexford put six goals by Laois and four by Waterford, and had two points to spare (1-8 to 1-6) over Tipperary in New Ross, but there was an 11 point defeat to Kilkenny in Nowlan Park and then the league campaign came to a sobering enough conclusion in Birr, when Offaly, underlining their performance in the championship the previous summer, went out of their way to win by eight points.

None of this hinted that Padge Kehoe and the boys were heading in the direction of another All-Ireland final, but that is where they ended up in September of 1970 after playing a large part in an historic year for the GAA. Eighty-minute games, for the first time in history, were thrown into the mix of provincial finals, and All-Ireland semi-finals and finals.

Galway were also thrown into the mix – after exiting the Munster championship after 11 years of trying and not getting anywhere down south.

Wexford had a 19 points victory over Dublin in the Leinster semi-final on June 22, Tony Doran getting two goals and also clipping over one point, but the Leinster final looked harder than ever to win – it was one thing holding out against Kilkenny for 60 minutes, but giving them an extra 20 minutes to stage one of their trusty resurrections meant that it was going to be a mercilessly long afternoon in the company of the Cats.

Wexford, indeed, had to bolt all doors and shutter all windows by the closing stages of the game.

Kilkenny laid siege on their goalmouth.

Wexford held a 14 points lead early in the second-half, and won by five (4-16 to 3-14) as Kilkenny threw everything they had at them, and also introduced flu victim Eddie Keher who had been unable to start. Altogether, Kilkenny hit Wexford for 2-10 in the second-half.

And for the final 10 minutes, as Pat Nolan was asked to make five quite miraculous saves, the notion of 80 minute games did not win many fans amongst those wearing the purple and gold on the field and also in the stands.

In the pages of *The Irish Independent*, John D Hickey expressed his concern thus for older gentlemen having to stretch their aged legs for an hour and 20 minutes:

'The distinction of winning the first senior championship hurling match of 80 minutes' duration was achieved by Wexford at Croke Park yesterday when they dethroned the All-Ireland champions Kilkenny, in a Leinster final that produced a satisfactory quota of skilful ball play despite an uncomfortably strong wind and the empirical efforts of several players to pace their game for entry into the unchartered regions of extended time.

It is almost impossible to make a balanced judgment of the 80-minute game on the evidence of an initial viewing. If the quality of the play is reasonably good, as it was yesterday, the new deal (an experiment in senior provincial finals and All-Ireland semi-finals and finals this year) certainly gives spectators sound value for their money.

As far as the players are concerned, the adjustment will take time. The younger men, generally, will stand the strain; but without judicious training and intelligent conservation of their energies, the older ones will wobble on rubber legs in the final stages of the fast match.

The Wexford full-back trio, Tom Neville, Mick Collins and Ned Colfer, all of whom were outstanding in the first-half yesterday, clearly showed the effects of the longer stint towards the end and as a result Kilkenny were presented with openings which could have brought disaster upon the challengers were it not for the splendid form of the goalkeeper, Pat Nolan, who made five great saves, all from close range, during the last 10 minutes.

The Older Kilkenny players such as Martin Coogan, Pa Dillon and Ted Carroll, also appeared to succumb to the demands of the clock, but gained more occasional relief than their opposite members because they enjoyed the help of the wind in the second-half.

Wexford's Phil Wilson, one of the oldest players afield, showed how the adjustment could be made, although playing in the stamina-devouring midfield position. Curbing his penchant for carrying the ball on solo runs, he invariably struck quickly after gaining possession and consequently played a major part in his team's success, slowing his pace only for a short period shortly after half-time... '

Hickey also went on record that Tony Doran had given Pa Dillon a 'nightmarish' 80 minutes. But for the second 40 minutes the supply of ball coming into the Wexford inside forwards did dry up.

Wexford had regained the Leinster title despite scoring only one goal and four points in that long and tiring second 40 minutes.

It did seem long... at that stage we were not used to it... it was a big change to move up from 60 minutes to 80 minutes. Adjusting from 60 to 80 was a big thing for every team, but the training was no different really.

The GAA brought it back to 70 minutes in 1975, which was more reasonable... it was a sensible compromise. In the league we were still playing 60 minutes in games... so, you can imagine... switching from playing a league game over 60 minutes, to a championship game over 80 minutes... it was a huge jump.

Especially at that time when there was less emphasis on fitness levels or anything else... 1970 was not like it is now, with players working out five and six times per week.

We didn't change anything we were doing in training that summer in 1970.

We were well on top in the first-half against Kilkenny... and then they came back at us in the second. No surprises there!

Phil Wilson... it was no bother to him in the middle of the field... Phil was a fitness fanatic, he could run all day long despite his age. A game over 80 minutes suited Phil just fine.

For the rest of us, it was a different matter I have to admit.

Quite how the new Leinster champions ended up playing Galway in the All-Ireland semi-final – and in Athlone, of all places – takes explaining.

Simply put, the game's bosses tripped over themselves.

It was felt that Galway had spent too long getting nowhere in Munster, and needed a reprieve. And when Congress sat over Easter it was quickly enough decided that Galway should be immediately airlifted out of the province.

Galway were happy to get out of the place, but in making their request they did not envisage receiving a ticket straight into the All-Ireland semi-final. Galway were equally happy to get out of Munster and then earn their place in the last four of the championship by beating somebody – either 'London-Irish' or some team from Ulster?

After that, Galway expected to meet the winners of the Leinster or Munster championships on a rotating basis. However, the Executive Committee of Central Council jumped the gun, and London-Irish and Galway were paired against the winners of the Munster and Leinster championships respectively.

The first semi-final was played in Limerick, the second semi-final in

Athlone, and both on the same afternoon. Getting back into the All-Ireland series after over a decade, Galway would have been prepared to make the longer trek and zip through Athlone on their way to Croke Park.

They felt a little disrespected, in truth.

And feeling put down by the authorities, the Galway team that showed up in Athlone was in the mood for a fight.

Wexford won by two points in the end, but the story of the game that ended 3-17 to 5-9, was pretty much all Galway and one man in the press box summed it up quite succinctly… *'Galway, the rank outsiders, the underdogs, who have been pushed around like an unwanted mongrel, took the honours of the day.'*

One writer described Wexford as *'inept'*.

Another writer asked why Wexford were *'over-confident'* when they had to line out without Phil Wilson, Willie Murphy and Ned Buggy from their Leinster final winning team?

Yet another said Wexford were plain *'lucky'*.

The story of the game?

Galway were 2-3 to 0-3 in front after 20 minutes thanks to goals from a Tom Ryan free and Bernie O'Connor.

That lead was down to a point by half-time after a 70-yard free from Dan Quigley was turned into the net by Tony Doran. But the former Tipperary and Clare player, Ryan, who would hold the upper hand on Quigley all day, and who finished up with 3-5 as a personal tally, did everything in his power to grab a last-minute goal and regain the lead.

It was what Galway deserved. Dan Quigley had grabbed an equaliser for Wexford from a '70' with seven minutes left on the clock. With three minutes left on the clock Dave Bernie had put Wexford in front for the first time.

We were blessed to get out of that ground… and get into the All-Ireland final. We never really got our heads around playing in Athlone.

It was a strange place to be for an All-Ireland semi-final.

They should have beaten us alright.

Maybe we thought we had some sort of divine right to get to play Cork in the final… I don't know. We knew Cork would be in the final.

I'd say we had our minds on Cork... that was the problem, and Galway fought for every single ball... didn't give us an inch.

If we thought we were big-shots at the beginning of that day, we didn't think it by the end.

Did not!

On September 7, their All-Ireland title hopes crashed down all around the Wexford team. They were resoundingly sent home with nothing to show for their year, Cork winning by 14 points (6-21 to 5-10).

You'd have to say with injuries and everything we went into that final as no-hopers... we could not afford to lose three players of their calibre.

I don't know if it was ill-tempered or so as games go... maybe there was a certain amount of niggly stuff in it alright.

We scored five goals in an All-Ireland final... and we were still beaten out the gate.

Strange thing.

John D Hickey had raised hopes in his preview to the game on the Saturday morning, recalling, in *The Irish Independent*, the giants of the game thus:

'To expect tomorrow's match to provide the splendid hurling of the counties' previous encounters is to hope for too much. The Rings and Rackards have passed by; we must be content with the offerings of lesser men. A comparison is unfair of course: giants are few in all games and it was fortuitous that so many were gathered together in the finals in the 1950s...'

But in his match report Hickey did not beat around the bush in getting to grips with the final, starting out thus:

'The shades of other days fell heavily and, perhaps, accusingly, across Croke Park yesterday. For the All-Ireland senior hurling final, which so many people had hoped would produce some of the splendour of the 1954 and 1956 deciders between Cork and Wexford, was a dismal flop, the Munster champions and national league title-holders winning their 21st championship crown with far more ease than their optimistic

supporters had dreamed of.

Expectation of a good game had been based on Wexford's reputation for producing the heroic rally when smitten by adversity. It had been known for some time that injuries would deprive them of the services of Willie Murphy, Phil Wilson and Ned Buggy in this encounter with Cork; but hope persisted that, once again, they would rise to the challenge and, at the very least, make their rivals battle all the way for the crown...'

John D Hickey had not turned his back on the bad feeling that coursed through the veins of the 1970 All-Ireland hurling final. He talked about... *'several nasty incidents, compromising false strokes, vicious pulling, rough tackles, deliberate provocation... and one player from each should have been sent off by referee Jimmy Hatton.'*

Wexford had put their best foot forward, and after Tony Doran had scored the first goal of the game in the fifth minute, it looked as though they would not back down from Cork's mighty presence.

But two minutes later Charlie McCarthy tapped over a point from a 21-yards free, another two minutes later Eddie O'Brien had another point from 25 yards, 90 seconds later Gerald McCarthy shot over a point from a 55-yards free, thirty seconds later O'Brien slammed home Cork's first goal from the edge of the square, two minutes later Gerald McCarthy was back on free duty and obliged from 65 yards, and then seven minutes passed until the next score of the game – another Cork point coming from Ray Cummins from 35 yards out.

Cork were in the mood.

And Cork never did flinch. They lifted Liam MacCarthy without ever looking over their shoulders.

Still.

A whole new, amazing decade awaited Wexford.

Tony Doran and his teammates had known All-Ireland final and league final victories and defeats in four tumultuous seasons – and there was no good reason why they would not continue to contend at the very top of the game, and deliver more memorable occasions for their hungry supporters.

Especially, when those same supporters looked through the Wexford team list on the day of the 1970 All-Ireland hurling final. The best years of the Wexford team, undoubtedly, lay before them.

In goals, Pat Nolan was 33 years old, but he was still one of the greatest goalkeepers in the country and nobody doubted his ability to hold down his position for another five or six years.

The full-back line was indeed creaking a little on the age front – Ned Colfer and Michael Collins were 29, and Tom Neville two years older.

Matt Browne was 28, Dan Quigley 25, and Teddy O'Connor just 24 on the half-back line; and in the middle of the field there was Dave Bernie (just 22) and Michael Jocob (just 24).

In front of them there was Martin Quigley (19), Pat Quigley (24), John Quigley (21), Mick Butler (20), Tony Doran (24), and Jack Berry (25). Wexford had youth on their side.

And the decade ahead held bountiful possibilities and opportunities.

However, there was still Kilkenny.

As there always was Kilkenny, from the very beginning of time.

The age of the team?

We may have looked a little old at the very back... but the rest... the remainder of the team was made up of young bucks!!!!

We may have thought we had the world at our feet... but, next door to us, we also had Kilkenny!!!!

Kilkenny won the next five Leinster finals against us... we went from young fellas in our mid-20s to old fellas! We did not think we had a right to be winning Leinsters and All-Irelands every year but... at the same time... we felt we'd be winning our share of them.

The majority of our team were just reaching their peak at that stage... still, it never happened for us.

We had a long wait... six years before we won again. All of those lads... all of us, 23 and 24 at that time in 1970, we were nearly 30 before we won the Leinster title again... and could fight for an All-Ireland.

When we played Cork again, in the All-Ireland final in '76... a third of us were 30 years of age or thereabouts.

We should have done more in the first half of the 70s, definitely. But we were well beaten in the Leinster final in '71, and we could have no complaints. In '72 there was a draw with Kilkenny in the Leinster final and halfway through the second-half... with 20 minutes to go we were 10 points up.

And Kilkenny were down to 14 men in that same game... and we still let them back to play a draw with us.

'73?

I don't know what went wrong in 1973... we'd won the league in '73... had played well, and then got into the Leinster final after beating a good Offaly team.

But Kilkenny suddenly peaked on that Sunday when everything was up for grabs.

'74?

Again, it was touch and go... they beat us by a point, but we were very unlucky to go down to 14 men when Phil Wilson, who was playing very well, was harshly sent-off on the stroke of half-time. Sadly, it turned out to be Phil's last appearance in a Wexford jersey after giving great service for almost a decade and a half.

'75?

They beat us again in a Leinster final... they seemed to edge it again... like they edged it so many times, but in the law of averages you would say we should have won two or three of those Leinster finals.

Wasn't so!

I'd say a couple of them..... in '71 we didn't do enough and in '73 we were blown out of it, but we could have won any of the others... if we had the rub of the green.

The 1974 final... Kilkenny won it with a last minute free... a very, very debatable free. And... y'know... '72... when we were 10 points up, we should have closed the game out... 6-13 each... we let them through for two or three goals in the last 10 minutes... should never have happened.

Probably, had we won that Leinster final in '72, which we could have had... the Kilkenny team that dominated the game for three or four years might never have had the same run at all.

Chapter 6

On August 4, 1957, Eddie Keher was a 15 years-old schoolboy playing minor for Kilkenny in the Leinster final. He slipped through for a couple of goals as Kilkenny took care of Offaly. Then he took his seat, and Keher, like everyone in Croke Park, prepared himself for a game between Wexford, two-time All-Ireland champions, and definitely Ireland's 'favourite' hurling team, against his own county.

Wexford were not just everyone's favourites – they were expected to dispense with Kilkenny en route to a hat-trick of All-Ireland titles – and a record fourth Leinster title in succession – having lifted Liam MacCarthy in 1955 and '56.

Wexford had rescued the game from a Munster stranglehold.

Of the 14 finals, before Wexford's All-Ireland triumph in 1955, eight had been won by Cork (who squeezed in a four in-a-row and a three in-a-row!) and Tipperary had journeyed home with Liam MacCarthy on four occasions.

Hurling folk simply loved Wexford.

There was no doubting that, because before Croke Park was rebuilt as one of the greatest stadiums in all of Europe, the three largest attendances at All-Ireland hurling finals had all involved a Wexford team – 77,854 in 1955 against Galway, 83,096 in 1956 against Cork, and 84,856 also against Cork in 1954. Over 51,000 spectators had turned up see the purple and gold in the 1955 All-Ireland semi-final against Limerick (12,000 more than the previous record for a semi-final).

Wexford, bottom line, were truly loved!

But in the 1957 Leinster final Wexford were sent scurrying out of sight after losing the Leinster final to Kilkenny.

It was not any loss.

It was a 6-9 to 1-5 loss.

There were giants on the hurling fields in the 1950s, and 60s and 70s, and there were giants who visited GAA grounds all over the country and placed their posteriors down in humble press boxes.

There were also giants on the sidelines!

Padge Kehoe was one such man who became larger than life in Wexford. And, in Kilkenny, there was a man in black, Fr Tommy Maher.

The 1957 Leinster final was Fr Tommy Maher's first as Kilkenny's maestro – and he would grow and grow as an influential leader of men in the two decades that followed. When he died in March of 2015, at 92 years of age, the full extent of Fr Tommy Maher's influence, and the reach of his magical teachings, only became fully known to hurling supporters all over the country.

Maher was Gowran-born, but his own hurling career was short lived because of his chosen religious path. He studied for the priesthood in Maynooth College and briefly worked as a curate in a parish in Dublin before being relocated to Kilkenny.

Lucky Kilkenny!

Maher would teach maths, physics and chemistry in St Kieran's College from 1963, and he would serve as president of the same college for 10 years from 1973. He then moved to Mullinavat, where as parish priest he breathed new life into the local hurling team.

After his death, Kilkenny hurling board chairman, the hard-working and inspirational Ned Quinn, tried his best to put the man's worth to the county into words. It was a job beyond even a man as irrepressible as Quinn. Fr Tommy had coached Kilkenny to 12 All-Ireland finals, of which they won seven.

'It might be hard for young people in Kilkenny nowadays to believe,' wrote Quinn. 'But when Paddy Grace invited Fr Tommy Maher to take charge of Kilkenny the county had not won a single All-Ireland in the previous 16 years.'

Quinn revealed Maher's brilliance as a teacher of hurling.

His excellence as a coach!

'He, Donie Nealon, John Hanley and Ned Power organised those courses (in Gormanston College in Meath in the 70s) which were the precursors to the present coaching systems in the GAA, but his interest in coaching went back even further than that. When he got involved in teams he realised that there could be a more scientific way to approach the game of hurling, that you could be cuter or cleverer and focus on the skills of the game and getting those right.'

Keher, who had watched Fr Tommy Maher at work in his first year with the Kilkenny team in 1957, had already met the man who would inspire him, and push him, during his schoolboy days in St Kieran's

'He was brilliant,' Keher would remember. 'It's hard to understand for young people today that there was little or no coaching in those days. Fr Maher was doing all the coaching that they do today back in the 1950s. He was analysing, isolating and outlining the skills of the game and devising practices to perfect them.

'He was a mathematician in his academic background, he taught me maths in St Kieran's. He had a mathematical mind; he'd be in his room weighing sliotars and looking at them, hurls too, and he'd work out what was the best way to do a skill and then he'd bring that to the training ground.'

It wasn't by accident that Tony Doran and his Wexford colleagues found themselves in a five-year spiral of defeats with Kilkenny at the beginning of the 1970s. The decade marked the final years of Fr Tommy Maher's days as Kilkenny coach and magician.

He would be gone by the middle of the decade.

And, in his absence, the Wexford team could breathe and round up greater ambition once again.

In the words of Tony Doran, a good 40 years later, those five years skipped by, but in truth there was more to it all than that.

They skipped by Wexford under instruction from a man with a white collar, Fr Tommy Maher.

That was a big score to concede in 1971, in the Leinster final... 6-16 ... a major score.

Kilkenny scored 5-8 in the second-half... which sounds unbelievable. On that occasion they took over in the second-half and blew us out of it. We had a respectable score in the second-half ourselves... enough to win most games.

The next year... '72... that was a game that could have changed the face of hurling during the 70s... had we seen it out when we were on top... but 6-13 each!

It was an incredible scoreline.

Then again... Wexford and Kilkenny... they were all high scoring games at that time.

It's hard to believe there was such a small crowd in Croke Park that afternoon... 18,000?

They were down to 14 men... and playing against the wind. Joe Murphy from Rathnure scored a point at the end to put us a point up and we were set to sneak it, but Mick Crotty got an equaliser out around the middle of the field.

We lost John Quigley who was injured in the sending off incident... and John was a massive loss to us at the time, but nevertheless, we should have seen it out. The second day was a good bit closer than the eight points on the scoreboard.

We had 14 wides in the first-half... too many, when we were on top. We'd led at half-time by a few points... but 14 wides... that's too much and Skehan made two great saves.

We dominated both days... they came strong in the last 15 minutes on each occasion.

That was the year we should have done it... definitely.

We had different people in charge of us during those five years.

I'm not sure if we had any manager or not at the start of the 70s, or if we only had four or five selectors.

In '73 Martin Doyle was manager and Nickey Rackard and Jim Morrissey were selectors with him. In '74 John Doyle was manager... a clubman of my own, and in '75 Syl Barron was manager.

Y'know, it looked like we were changing every year on the sideline.... but it was more or less the same group of players the whole time. Maybe we needed more continuity in personnel on the sideline... I don't know.

It might have helped us.

Padraig Puirseal, like John D Hickey, was one of the giants in the press box. Puirseal wrote for the *Irish Independent's* biggest rival, *The Irish Press* which closed its doors in the early summer of 1995 for good. But, for decades, the judgment of both men was taken as solid gold by GAA folk all over the country.

The pair were also born in two counties that fought it out on the hurling field, shoulder to shoulder, since the beginning of time. Hickey was born in Tipp, Puirseal in Mooncoin, in Kilkenny, in 1914, though Puirseal was a man who did not limit his pen to Gaelic football and hurling matches. After leaving UCD in the 1930s he would write four novels, beginning with *Hanrahan's Daughter* in 1942, a story of romance and hurling and a work translated into several different languages, before getting to work on a trilogy of novels – *A Keeper of Swans* (1944), *The Quiet Man* (1946), and *Fiddler's Green* (1949). At the time he was also writing for booklets and magazines, keeping the name of Patrick Purcell on all of his non-GAA writing. He wrote for *Gaelic Weekly* under the pen name *Rambling Rory*. For 30 years he penned a *Dublin Letter* for the *Kilkenny People*, and he also contributed to a weekly programme on Radio Eireann. He was employed briefly at the *Independent* before crossing the river Liffey and taking his desk at the *Press*.

Like John D Hickey, Puirseal had a big say in the selection of the All Star teams, that were introduced in 1971, and he remained on the selection committee until his death in September of 1979, four months before he was due to retire from the newspaper business. The 1978 All-Ireland football final between Kerry and Dublin had been Padraig Puirseal's one hundredth to attend.

Puirseal watched from the Hogan Stand, pen and notebook in front of him, as Wexford let a 1-9 to 1-8 half-time lead slip in the 1971 Leinster final, and Kilkenny swiftly moved up the gears thereafter to win by 6-16 to 3-16. It was a game in which Tony Doran's goal rate dropped to just one for the day. He had scored two in the defeat of Offaly in the Leinster semi-final.

It was a stinging defeat for Wexford because, twice in the league they had laid down a marker against the Cats – defeating them in Wexford Park by three points (2-12 to 2-9) in March, and enforcing their superiority in Waterford two months later in a league play-off, winning by one (5-8 to 3-13) in a right thriller.

That battle took a lot out of Wexford as they were over-run by Clare (4-10 to 1-7) a week later in the league quarter-final.

The 1971 Leinster final was played on July 11, and Padraig Puirseal saw his native county make small work of being rank outsiders. Puirseal wrote in *The Irish Press* about the final thus:

'The Leinster senior hurling title and the massive O'Keeffe Cup are both back in Kilkenny after the Noremen's surprisingly clear-cut victory in yesterday's Croke Park final which, if it provided 41 scores, some superb individual performances and quite a few memorable moments, yet fell well short of the high all-round standard of hurling excellence and thrilling exchanges that we have so rightly come to expect from provincial finals between these two counties.

This was a game in which brilliant efforts and downright scrappy hurling seemed to alternate, a game in which Kilkenny, the outsiders on pre-match reckoning, called the tune almost all the way, except for a disastrous spell in the six minutes before the interval when they let a five-point lead slip away so that they trailed at half-time by a point, 1-8 to 1-9.

But this was a title that may well have been won and lost in the dressing rooms during the interval.

Christy Jacob did not reappear in the Wexford line-out for the second-half. Instead, Vinny Staples, long absent from inter-county hurling, came on at left half-back. The Slaneyside mentors also transferred Colm Doran to right half-forward to mark Martin Coogan and sent Christy Kehoe who had provided many first-half problems for Coogan, to the left wing to try and contain Pat Lalor, who had been Kilkenny's outstanding defender through those first 40 minutes.

Meanwhile, the Kilkenny selectors, obviously perturbed by a sluggish first half showing forward, despite the excellent chances provided, reshuffled their attack, only the left wing of Eddie Keher and Eddie Byrne retained their original positions.

And the real story of that second half, and of Kilkenny's comfortable victory, is that Kilkenny's second thoughts proved completely effective, while the Wexford moves backfired.

Christy Kehoe tried hard, but Pat Lalor, the man of this match for my money, continued to hurl as though he owned the ball, while not alone did Colm Doran do little to impair Coogan's customary efficiency but his departure from defence left the whole Wexford rearguard at sixes and sevens. Moreover, the winners' Mossy Murphy from Mullinavat, when moved to centre-forward, proved far more effective there than his captain Paddy Delaney had been.

Yet, though Kilkenny, greatly aided by a Murphy goal almost directly after the restart continued to make the running, Wexford, now aided by the blazing sun and the slight breeze, were level again after seven minutes of the second half.

Next, a long free from Martin Coogan sailed all the way to the Wexford net, and then, after an exchange of points, came the two minutes that ended any further speculation about the outcome.

Wexford, a goal in arrears, were awarded a 21-yard free. Christy Kehoe's shot hit a post, and the rebound was cleared to Colm Doran who clipped over a point.

From the puck-out, Wexford stormed back to the attack. Ollie Walsh caught a high ball as it dropped on his posts, sidestepped one forward, then another, soloed out to the 21 and unleashed an immense clearance upfield. Eddie Byrne, racing out, whipped up the ball, rounded Matt Browne and drove home Kilkenny's fourth and decisive goal.

From this body blow Wexford wilted steadily until they were 12 points in arrears with as many minutes left for play.......'

In the six Leinster finals (including one drawn game) in the first-half of the 1970s, Kilkenny outscored Wexford on pure goals by 27-17. While some of the matches over those five years between 1971 and '75 were mercilessly tight, there is no getting away from the fact that the Cats managed to hit the net when it mattered most. In those six games, Tony Doran's strike rate with goals was three. He totaled 3-13 in the six games, which was below his average.

Wexford also led at half-time in three of those six games (in 1971, and both games in '72) but the fact of the matter was that Kilkenny, lethal to the very bone, were of a mind to finish games harder and stronger than their opposition.

Fr Tommy Maher knew that the third 'quarter' in games was most often the defining 'quarter'. And 1972 provided ample evidence of how Kilkenny knew when games were there to be won.

In the big-scoring Leinster final in 1972, which would end 6-13 each, Kilkenny had been 3-7 to 4-7 in arrears at the change of ends. In the replay they were five points behind at the change, 0-6 to 1-8. In the second-half of the two games, they struck for 3-6 and 3-10 respectively – and in the Leinster finals that followed Kilkenny never let up in the second-half, scoring 2-11 in 1973, 3-5 in '74, and 1-8 in '75.

Three times Kilkenny brought home the Liam MacCarthy Cup in those five years, and as Tony Doran knew in his heart, three of those five years might have belonged to Wexford.

Were Kilkenny smarter, more cunning?

It would appear so.

The Leinster final of 1972, in fact, was presented in the daily newspapers as the defining meeting between the two counties. Each had claimed the provincial crown twice in the previous four years.

In the semi-finals, Kilkenny had struggled in holding off a brave Laois effort, shipping five goals but getting through by 5-14 to 5-7 in the end. In comparison, Wexford had it relatively easy against Dublin, coasting home by 4-13 to 2-5.

'Changes by the Wexford selectors have now provided the Wexford team with a middle line that looks impressively strong and experienced from full-back to full-forward, with Tom Neville, John Quigley, Phil Wilson, Martin Quigley, Tony Doran and Jack Berry manning the key positions. Assisted by able men on the wings, this axis will demand something more than the ordinary from Kilkenny, if the 1971 All-Ireland finalists are to retain the Bob O'Keeffe Cup.'

That was the view of John D Hickey in *The Irish Independent.*

In the pages of *The Irish Times*, furthermore, Paddy Downey was questioning the decision by Fr Tommy Maher and his colleagues to place

Fan Larkin at No.3.

'*Some doubts have been expressed about the wisdom of the Kilkenny selectors in placing diminutive Fan Larkin at full back, where John Walsh, a replacement for the retired Pa Dillon, was not a success against Laois. My own opinion is that the great hearted Larkin will not be found wanting in his new role for the county and that his display will inspire a defence whose half-back line has the strength to contain much of Wexford's attacking thrust.*'

A game that contained 12 goals and 26 points equally divided between two teams, which was the end result of the 1972 Leinster hurling final, did not warm the toes of everybody, however.

Padraig Puirseal in *The Irish Press* was picky about what he had viewed, explaining his feeling thus:

'*While one must preface comment on the proceedings by saying that the game did not produce vintage hurling, it did give to the disappointing attendance of 18,611 an enthralling finish, as Kilkenny overcame the handicap of playing for all but 17 minutes of the second half with 14 men – after Mick Brennan was sent to the sideline for a foul on John Quigley when there were still 23 minutes remaining and at a time when Kilkenny were trailing by two goals, and playing against the wind.*

While their deficit was moderate enough, such had been the trend of events that it seemed inconceivable that Kilkenny could save their title.

Indeed, had Wexford not wasted some excellent opportunities to add to their total, Kilkenny's peril would have been infinitely greater, before the champions found in adversity the spur to splendid endeavour.

The departure of Brennan seemed to signal the end for Kilkenny, but where previously there had been mediocrity, the team was inbued with a new wave of determination that ran through the ranks and they gradually eroded Wexford's advantage in a manner worthy of champions.'

With 90 seconds remaining on the clock the sides were level at 6-12 each.

Then Joe Murphy, who had come into the game in the third minute for the injured Pat Flynn, knocked over what appeared to be the winning point.

Kilkenny's brave rally appeared to have been in vain.

But Mick Crotty grabbed the draw.

In the replay, Wexford held a 1-8 to 0-6 advantage at half-time, and they had also sent the ball wide 14 times. They looked in control, despite their wastefulness. Padraig Puirseal explained what happened next:

'Shrewdness on the sideline can play a major part in the happenings on the field, and yesterday a switch after 10 minutes of the second half that brought Pat Delaney from centre half-forward to full-forward, paid a handsome dividend.

Within two minutes of his advent to the edge of the square, Delaney shot a great goal that brought Kilkenny back into the game that appeared to be slipping away and it cut Wexford's six-points lead to three. More important, however, it shattered the composure of a defence that had, up to that point, contained everything Kilkenny had to offer, with centre half-back Mick Jacob marshalling his colleagues in excellent fashion and setting the tenor by precept and example...

Even allowing for what was on occasion a prodigious waste of scoring chances, Wexford's advantage would have been more but for two magnificent saves by Noel Skehan in the Kilkenny goal, and many times during a distinguished career Kilkenny have had reason to be grateful for the redoubtable qualities of left corner-back Jim Treacy.

This was yet another, for the Bennettsbridge defender was the anchor for a defence that was, during the first period, distinctly uneasy against a half-forward line that played with fire and method, none more so than centre-forward Tony Doran, but did not reap the tangible benefit because of inaccuracy, and a slightly cumbersome full-forward line.'

The Leinster final replay ended Kilkenny 3-16, Wexford 1-14.

Kilkenny would also end up All-Ireland champs in 1972.

The conveyor-belt that served the game of hurling in Kilkenny so impressively did not slow down in years that ended with All-Ireland titles. There were always younger men, stronger men sometimes it seemed, appearing in the black and amber.

Pa Dillon played his last heroic game for Kilkenny in September of 1972, when a spectacular final 20 minutes rudely stopped Cork in their tracks. By that time, Cork had worked themselves into a 5-11 to 1-15 lead but, as Tony Doran and Wexford had experienced on so many occasions – and would have to continue living with – Kilkenny then turned the game on its head, and went about claiming the Liam MacCarthy Cup for the 18th time.

The Cats scored 2-9 in the final 20 minutes of the game.

Over that same period of time, Cork got nothing at the other end of the field, which was down to the stubborn qualities of Dillon, Pat Henderson in front of him, and also substitute Martin Coogan.

Pa Dillon would end his career with four All-Ireland medals. In the 1972-73 season he appeared in some of Kilkenny's early league games, and was called back into the Kilkenny squad at the beginning of the championship in '73, but did not get any game time. Instead, there was a new name now in the No.3 jersey, and blending into a defence featuring Skehan, Larkin, Treacy, Lawlor, Henderson and Morrissey, as if he had been born to take such a place in life.

Nicky Orr from The Fenians, however, did not come from a long Kilkenny line. His father, Joe was a native of Glencar in Donegal and came to Kilkenny as an army recruit during 'The Emergency' of the 1940s. Joe Orr would marry a Johnstown woman, Theresa Grace and their son, Nicky would end up captaining an All-Ireland winning Kilkenny team. Before that, however, Nicky Orr was Pa Dillon's understudy for two years before getting his big chance.

Orr, more a bull of a man than Dillon, would not be all that long in the famous No.3, playing his last championship game in the 1976 Leinster final when Wexford put in a performance which stated that the county had finally had enough of losing to Kilkenny – winning the game by 17 points. But in his four seasons, Orr would do more than his part in helping to bring home two more All-Ireland titles, in 1974 and '75.

Nicky Orr came up against Tony Doran for the first time in a championship match in the 1973 Leinster final. But he also fought it out under the high ball against Doran twice in the league, in Wexford Park in early December in '72 when the visitors won by 10 points (3-16 to 3-6) and then again in the league semi-final in Waterford in April when just a single point divided the two teams, Wexford edging it 2-10 to 2-9, and making their way through to the final where they would meet a high-flying and exciting Limerick team that would be crowned All-Ireland champions by the end of the same year.

Getting a bit of a whipping by Wexford in the league final, losing by nine points (4-13 to 3-7), actually helped fortify Limerick and build them into a team ready to fight all the harder for the All-Ireland prize.

A league title in '73 was the only major reward for Wexford for five years of often magnificent hurling. They deserved more.

We could have won more Leinster titles... another All-Ireland in that time, I have no doubt about that at all... but in all of those games we did everything we could do to win... every single one of them.

Yah... you could say we were unlucky, but you could also say that the best teams make their own luck on the biggest days.

We showed that we were every bit as good as Limerick in '73... better than them at the start of the summer, certainly, but we lost the Leinster that year by 10 points. We were well behind at half-time against Kilkenny, and never were able to cut back on their lead.

We were good enough, I'd say, to win the All-Ireland in '73, I'd say we were, but... we weren't good enough to beat Kilkenny.

Wexford got their league campaign off to a flyer, hitting Tipperary for 4-15 and winning by 12 points in New Ross. They beat Offaly, lost to Kilkenny, but then in the new year overcame Cork and Clare in February. Another big score, 4-14 was put up against Galway in a 19-point victory, but then they lost to Limerick in Enniscorthy, 4-11 to 2-12. There were two matches against Waterford, the first drawn, before the semi-final win over Kilkenny.

John D Hickey of *The Irish Independent* saw Wexford and Limerick, who were appearing in their fourth successive final, fight long and hard, and sometimes with a meanness of spirit, in the 1973 league decider. Limerick were in big trouble by half-time, 10 points down and sinking, after goals from Tony Doran, Tom Byrne and Martin Quigley.

Mossie Dowling and Eamonn Cregan grabbed a brace of Limerick goals on the restart, but these were casually cancelled out by Tom Byrne and Doran who finished, between them, with the splendid tally of 3-8.

Hickey wrote thus of Wexford's commanding 4-13 to 3-7 win:

'While injury-smitted Wexford richly merited their victory over Limerick in a tempestuous National Hurling league final at Croke Park yesterday, it might, in all reason, be contended that the comparatively unsightly sight of the scoreboard was not a true reflection of the throbbing entertainment content of the contest.

Wexford's glorious finish, which was in entire accord with their performance right through the hour, brought 1-2 in the last two minutes, thus giving the game a rather one-sided appearance to the ill-advised who stayed away.

In hurling accomplishment, it did not come up to the standard of the other league final between the two counties – the 1958 decider, which the Leinster county won by 5-7 to 4-8 – but despite that circumstance it was a battle royal.

Wexford, it is imperative to put on record, contributed much more than the opposition to the sparkling spectacle, but Limerick earned more than a nod of praise for never accepting that they were doomed to defeat.

However, let those who would belittle Limerick reflect for a moment, or for an hour or more, and come up with any team of recent times that would not have withered in the increasing intensity of the opposition's supercharged display.

From the brilliant goalkeeper Pat Nolan, who figured on the side who defeated Limerick in the 1958 league decider, right up to left corner-forward Jack Berry, it was a case of Wexford having a super-abundance of power...

Time and again Limerick altered the disposition of their forces, but it astonished me they never made the switch of which they seemed most in need, the transfer of Pat Hartigan to full-back instead of Eamon Rea, who found Tony Doran a mystery beyond his comprehension...

After an opening of bewildering fluidity, Limerick had the first score of the game, a point from a free by Richie Bennis in the fourth minute. Two minutes later Grimes had a glorious point and Wexford opened their account in the eight minute with a point from a free by Tom Byrne.

After Bennis had another point free in the 12th minute, Wexford cascaded forward and had three scores in the space of three minutes – Christy Keogh a point in the 13th, a point from Byrne to level in the 14th, and then a goal by Tony Doran.

Grimes temporarily stopped the rot with a point in the 17th minute and then again came whirlwind Wexford with scores by Byrne, a goal in the 18th minute, points by Martin Quigley and Byrne (free) in the 20th and 23rd minutes, a goal by Tony Doran in the 24th and a point free by Ned Buggy in the 25th minute. Two minutes before the break, Bennis pointed a Limerick free to leave the interval score – Wexford 3-6, Limerick 0-5...'

Two more goals from Tony Doran in the Leinster semi-final, in a five-point win (2-14 to 2-9) over Offaly in Nowlan Park, led to another mini-epic against Kilkenny in the Leinster final.

This time, Kilkenny did not wait around when the ball was thrown in, and by half-time they led 2-11 to 0-9. They neatly doubled their tally in the second-half, winning the provincial crown by 4-22 to 3-15.

Tony Doran got a single point.

Nicky Orr, in the process, showed himself to be made of the right stuff – and made of the same stuff as those who had come before in the Kilkenny No.3 shirt. In the press box, John D Hickey was still watching.

'The state of the scoreboard at the call of time – 4-22 to 3-15 in favour of Kilkenny – did scant justice to the superiority of the All-Ireland title-holders as they pulverised the challenge of National league winners Wexford at Croke Park yesterday in a Leinster senior hurling championship final, all the delights and delicacies of which were provided by the victors.

Kilkenny hurled joyously as they romped through the 80-minute decider but generously though they decorated the tie, it was insipid in comparison with some of the thundering provincial finals we have seen between the counties in modern times. The winners did all anyone could expect from one side to hallmark the event, but unhappily the black and amber jerseys did not fire Wexford with the customary response on this occasion.

The state of the parties at the end and a total of 44 scores, a rate of more than one every two minutes, might readily be interpreted by those not at the game as indicative of a rip-roaring struggle. But such was not the case...

Were I a Kilkenny supporter I feel sure that when the first surge of pride in the triumph had subsided the main boost I would find in reflection on the match would be the performance of up to yesterday unproven full-back Nicky Orr. He played no less a man than Tony Doran right out of the match and in the final minutes even more comprehensively underminded the rating of Jack Berry.

Doran had only one point, but even more important from a Kilkenny viewpoint was the fact that the Buffers Alley man, a torment of full-backs, never looked even remotely likely to score a goal or even make one. If this was the real Orr, Kilkenny officialdom can blithely let the great Pa Dillon go into retirement he so keenly wishes without any pangs that he might be letting the side down.'

Chapter 7

Pat Nolan would finally call it a day, and take his leave of his position between the Wexford goalposts in 1974. It was a place that he had come to own, which was an amazing achievement in itself since back in the mid-50s, the Oylegate man was patiently sitting on the Wexford substitutes bench, waiting his turn.

It wasn't any old wait, however.

Nolan was waiting for the magnificent Art Foley to call it a day. Foley, who had been so often the hero of the day in 1955 and '56, who had made a breathtaking save from Christy Ring in the latter final – a save that GAA historians are regularly united in terming the greatest save in the history of the game – had emigrated with his wife, Anne and their three young children to the east coast of the United States in 1957 and would eventually settle into a quiet life on Long Island and a career in the airline industry.

While Pat Nolan proceeded to become one of the greatest Wexford goalkeepers of all time and seriously rival his predecessor, Art Foley was pretty much forgotten; but Foley was living a full and rewarding life, raising six children in total, and enjoying his grandchildren and great grandchildren.

His fellow workers were never to know that Foley was a sporting hero, and even Wexford folk living on the east coast of the US did not realise that the great Art Foley was amongst them until almost 60 years had passed since his decision to emigrate.

In 2015, over 150 Wexford people finally had the great honour of 'honouring' the famous man. 'After receiving a call from Wexford hurling supporter club leader, Joe Carroll in January of this year, I had to go through several channels to determine where Art lived and if he was still with us,' Wexford Association president, John Murphy explained to the *Enniscorthy Guardian*. In a night of memories, Foley had Irish Consulate General, Barbara Jones, a native of Enniscorthy like Art Foley himself, turn up and pay her respects. The majority leader of New York's City Council, Jimmy Van Bramer, whose grandmother also came from Wexford, also paid his respects.

Video tributes came from Wexford's 1996 All-Ireland winning captain, Martin Storey and another survivor from the brilliant 50s, Ned Wheeler. 'It was a beautiful thing you did Art,' Wheeler stated, remembering Foley's incredible save from Ring in the 1956 final, 'not only for yourself, your teammates, but all the Wexford people down the years.'

Pat Nolan had been Foley's understudy in '56, when he won his first Celtic Cross. Nolan had nailed down the position as his own in 1958, proved imperious in 1960 when Wexford put down Tipperary in the All-Ireland final, 2-15 to 0-11 – in a game in which his brother, John made his championship debut and kept Jimmy Doyle scoreless – and Pat was still there for the '62 and '65 defeats by Tipperary, and the 1970 loss to Cork, but in between all of this he had won his third All-Ireland medal in 1968. He also had his three National league medals in his back pocket before retiring at 37 years of age.

Nolan would be named by Eddie Keher on his greatest team of all time (excluding Kilkennymen). 'He was unspectacular,' Keher commented, 'but a great reader of the game and a shot-stopper.' But in the 1974 Leinster final, six of the best Kilkenny goals went by Pat Nolan.

In every way, '74 was one of the truly epic contests between the neighbouring counties – eight goals in total, and just one agonising point between the teams on the final whistle. It was a four in-a-row for the Cats in Leinster, but they were fortunate, and helped by the fact that Offaly referee, Mick Spain dismissed Phil

Wilson for an incident right on the stroke of half-time. It did not help Wexford either that Spain called a halt to the game with 20 seconds remaining on the stop watches of some of the giants in the press box.

In the pages of *The Irish Times*, Paddy Downey was perplexed.

'Kilkenny have done what no other county has done, won four Leinster Senior Hurling titles in successive years. But the manner of that achievement in Croke Park yesterday was very much less than satisfactory as their rivals, Wexford, fought with tenacity to overcome a series of crippling blows to their morale only to see a man well accustomed to the role, Eddie Keher, execute the telling blow for Kilkenny from a free, leaving the champions victors by one point from an incredible tally for both teams of 61 points.

While the ultimate victory belonged to Kilkenny, the sympathy of the attendance of 20,742 was overwhelmingly with Wexford, who had only 14 men on duty for the entire second period, and despite that fact dominated the exchanges with hardly a break throughout forty minutes of fiercely competitive hurling, which is unlikely to be equalled for sheer tension for a long time to come.

The second half may – and no one will want to further the anguish which must have been felt by the Wexford team and supporters at the end – have been twenty seconds short. When referee, Mick Spain of Offaly, sounded the final whistle, there was, according to two stop-watches in the press box, that much time remaining and, as Wexford were in possession at that stage, it can be a matter of conjecture only as to whether the losers might have summoned up an equaliser.

The rate of scoring throughout the game and in the second half particularly, suggests that they would...'

Eight goals scored on an afternoon in Croke Park, and Tony Doran's name was not on any of them. The Buffers Alley man shot four points. He had chances, but Kilkenny were mightily fed up of watching Doran breaking down their defence and coming away with goals.

As far as the Kilkenny dressing-room was concerned – and he was the most discussed man in that room most of the time – Doran needed to be stopped at all costs. Furthermore, Kilkenny felt that if Doran was denied goals, then they should always beat Wexford.

Simple as that.

I had my chances, but always seemed to be bottled up... one of those days, I suppose.

It's funny, when you look back... there were matches when I might have a chance to get 10 goals, and score a couple and, then... other matches I'd be lucky to get one good clear chance at goal.

That Leinster final in '74 was one of those games, if I remember.

But Kilkenny were fierce determined that year. They were hungry for another All-Ireland. I wouldn't say they were any hungrier than us, but... they wanted it badly.

And they won the All-Ireland in '74... then won it again in '75. The newspapers were saying that they were one of the greatest hurling teams of all time.

Certainly, most of the men who played on the Kilkenny team of the 70s have gone down in the game's history books as legends of the game. And, rightly or wrongly, more Kilkenny hurlers are given that status than Wexford hurlers of the same period. One of those Kilkenny men was 'Fan' Larkin.

The story of the Larkin family more than most other families, perhaps, tells the story of Kilkenny hurling and its power, and the ability of the county to repeatedly produce outstanding teams. 'Fan' Larkin was christened Philip Larkin, like the famed poet, but he was called 'Fan' around the yard at home so that he was distinguishable from a cousin of the same name.

Fan's father, Paddy won All-Ireland medals in 1932, '33 and '35, and also in the 'Thunder and Lightning' final in 1939 – the monstrous September day in which the Second World War broke out. He was Kilkenny captain in 1936 when they lost the All-Ireland final to the magic and grace of Mick Mackey's Limerick, and he was also leading the Cats in '38 when they were surprised by Dublin in a Leinster final.

Fan himself won a handful of All-Ireland medals as well, in 1963, '72, '74, '75 and '79; the final one against Galway when he was 38 years of age. And Fan's son, Philly, keeping up the majestic James Stephens' tradition, was part of Brian Cody's first two All-Ireland victories as manager of Kilkenny in 2000 and '02.

In the 1975 Leinster final, Kilkenny made sure that it wasn't a nail-biter like '74, earning a four points advantage at half-time and winning by six.

Paddy Downey saw it thus:

Say no more about Dad's Army and its exploits, good or bad, on many fields. We live in the time of Grandad's Armada (alias Kilkenny), a celebrated force that blithely defies the passage of the years. It was a breathtaking sight to see it in full sail at Croke Park yesterday, buffeted severely at times, within inches of foundering once or twice, but graceful always and ultimately sweeping onwards to another magnificent conquest. Forgive a writer's search for metaphors and images to describe the course and the result of the Leinster hurling final at GAA headquarters; something more than ordinary praise expressed in ordinary language is needed to tell the story of Kilkenny's victory over Wexford.

Five of the winning team – Larkin, Henderson, Delaney, Purcell and Keher – have turned 30; several of the others are not far off that mark, but in concert they looked like young colts, defying not only the powerful challenge offered by Wexford but also the fierce heat of a blazing afternoon to beat their own record with a fifth successive provincial triumph...

It was a tough game, so tough that little room was left for the finer examples of hurling, though these flashed through the grim battle occasionally. It was volatile, too, almost to the point of explosion at times in the first half, but in spite of such fierce pulling and a few reckless strokes, sportsmanship gained the day...

But the necessary scores did come for the challengers for whom Tony Doran, whose strong hurling made Kilkenny's great centre half-back Pat Henderson look quite ordinary, set up several openings. But, then, when it seemed that Wexford would make the vital breakthrough, Doran was inexplicably moved to full-forward and Kilkenny held on for a four point interval lead.

At the start of the second half, Doran was back on the 40 in an attack which was switched around beyond recognition during the remainder of the game. John Quigley, for instance, was moved to four different positions and played with all his might in each of them, but he was asked to do too much, and asked too much of himself.

His brother, Martin did much to repair the uneven state of affairs at midfield when he moved out from right half-forward just before half-time, and this was reflected in the struggle after the change of ends, six points being shared equally in the first 12 minutes.

Then came the score which could have won the game for Wexford, a wonderful goal by Doran who, gaining possession from John Murphy's pass through sent a mighty drive from 14 yards range whistling past Noel Skehan.

That left the challengers only one point behind – 2-11 to 1-15. They had now taken the game by the scruff of the neck and, with Kilkenny faltering all over the field, seemed set to regain the provincial crown for the first time since 1970. But inaccuracy again halted their onslaught. Doran drove another fierce shot across the posts with Skehan vulnerable, then missed the chance of a point for the equaliser, and Buggy sent a free puck wide from long range.

But what really raised the siege was a magnificent point by Kilkenny's Kieran Purcell who, from a puck out, caught the ball in a cluster of players on his own 50 yards line and with scarcely a pause swung it straight between the posts for a lead of two points...

Just one minute after his vital point, Keher seemed insane when he telegraphed his intention of shooting for a goal from a 'semi-penalty'. But his gamble succeeded, fortunately for the champions, when the ball spun marginally over the line off the Wexford goalkeeper's hurley. That score gave Kilkenny a lead of 2-16 to 2-11 with 15 minutes remaining...

It ended 2-20 to 2-14, and Eddie Keher duly collected his tenth Leinster medal. Wexford had five years of defeats to Kilkenny to pour over and analyse, but in the winter of 1975 they surely realised that they had inadvertently helped Kilkenny on their way to a second All-Ireland on the trot, and potentially to a famous three in-a-row.

Wexford had six men making the crucial decisions on the sideline that day on August 3, 1975; and crucially they had failed to come to grips with maximising the impact of the Doran brothers – Colm was moved to centre-back to nullify the effects of Kieran Purcell, but it didn't work as planned, and Tony was strangely moved to the edge of the square and into the company of Nicky Orr, when he was already giving Pat Henderson more to think about than the veteran Kilkenny great cared for.

A young Brian Cody played his part in the Kilkenny defence, but with Wexford shooting an abysmal total of 19 wides by the end of the afternoon, the Cats defenders could not be totally content with their own work.

Though, after dethroning champions Limerick in the 1974 All-Ireland final (3-19 to 1-13) and then accounting for Galway with 10 points to spare in

September of '75 (2-22 to 2-10), there were not that many Kilkenny hurlers being kept awake at night with any regrets during the following winter.

For Brian Cody, life was good.

He was playing amongst giants in the Kilkenny defence, and he was voted onto the Allstar team at the end of 1975. In Kilkenny, the view was that the county should already have been sitting on three Liam MacCarthy Cups in-a-row during the winter of '75.

In his autobiography, *Cody*, published in 2009, Brian Cody recounted that 1973's loss to Limerick felt like a missed opportunity. 'The general view in Kilkenny – and outside too – was that if we hadn't been hit with such a serious injury blitz in 1973, the All-Ireland treble would have been secured a year before. And since we won again in '75, there's every possibility that a four-timer would have been achieved. Then again, you never know.

'Sport is fickle and who knows how the landscape might have changed if Kilkenny had won in '73. As it was, we were pushed to the very limit by Wexford in the 1974 Leinster final, winning by a point in one of those remarkably high scoring games where it was difficult to keep track as the goals and points flew in.'

Cody's club, James Stephens or the 'The Village' as they are commonly known, also were Kilkenny champions by the end of 1975 – so Cody had All-Ireland under-21 and senior medals, as well as a Kilkenny medal, to count out on his sideboard that winter. He remembers that time as the first occasion that he came up against and saw exactly what sort of man Tony Doran was.

'By now, of course, the All-Ireland club championships were gathering momentum and, since it was the first time The Village had played in them, it represented a new and exciting challenge which would take us all the way to the final against Blackrock in Thurles the following May. We were lucky enough to get that adventure off to a successful start, having had a really tough battle with Buffers Alley in the first round game down in Wexford Park.

'It was one of my first battles with Tony Doran, who lined out at centre-forward. He was a phenomenal player with the heart of a lion and the strength of an ox. On top of that, he had an amazing capacity to create a chute for high balls to drop into his great big hand. Once he got the ball, his strength and courage took over as he turned and drove towards goal. I had a great battle with him in that particular provincial club game which we won by a few points.'

Life looked even sweeter for Cody and Co when they continued their winning ways in 1976, finally lifting the league title after a couple of replays against Cork and Clare in June.

'We were All-Ireland and National league champions,' Cody recalled, 'confidence levels were high and everything was in place for a crack at the championship three in-a-row.

'Sure, what on earth could go wrong?'

Chapter 8

On a Saturday afternoon in April, 1976, a few days after Wexford had drawn with Clare (2-9 to 3-6) in the National league semi-final, Nickey Rackard was in his hospital bed at St Vincent's Hospital on the south side of Dublin reading his copy of *The Irish Field*. He was awaiting a visit from his wife, Ailish and his son, Bobby and two daughters, Marion and Bernadette. The same afternoon, Nickey Rackard, the greatest Wexford hurler there ever was, died.

It was alcoholism that brought the brilliant, swash-buckling hero to his knees more than once in his life; it was cancer that ended his life all too soon at 54 years of age. It was known that Rackard was running out of time, but, always a man of courage, he told family and friends that he was not afraid of dying. He had enjoyed many years of sobriety. He was a contented man in his final years, right to the very end. And he spent the last few precious years of his life helping others, who, just like him, had their lives crushed by their need for alcohol.

Because of his fame, and his honesty, people from all over the country called to Nickey Rackard's home for a quick word, or some longer counselling. It is said that some stayed for days.

'I think as a family,' his son, Bobby recalled in 2005, when the GAA dedicated a cup to his memory, one aimed at giving weaker counties a leg up in life, '… that's the legacy we would be most proud of.'

As a young boy, Bobby and his sisters observed their father's drinking become progressively worse, but Nickey Rackard always remained a caring and loving Dad. Nickey was a Wexford selector in 1968 when the county took down mighty Tipperary, and he made sure that his son was with him in the dugout, sitting amongst the Wexford substitutes, during the course of that memorable game.

But the home of an alcoholic is still the home of an alcoholic.

'In an alcoholic home,' Bobby Rackard told *The Sunday Independent*, 'it's like you feel you're in the trenches to a certain extent. There's a system of operating that becomes established. In dysfunctional homes there's a lot of tension, a lot of fear, it's a difficult emotional lifestyle.

'I don't think he realised, or society in general realised, the damage that drink can do. I don't know what sort of attitudes to drink existed at the time, it seemed a sort of manly thing.'

Nickey Rackard's difficulties with drink had begun while he was studying to be a veterinarian in Dublin. It took him over eight years to complete his degree, but he got there, despite his sacrifices in the name of the Wexford team and his other distractions. But in 1951 he took the pledge and signed up with the Pioneer Total Abstinence Association, and when Wexford won back-to-back All-Irelands in 1955 and '56 there was no question of Nickey Rackard taking a drink.

In New York, on a hurling visit the following year, Rackard began drinking again, and he became embroiled in a desperate battle for the next 12 years, before he once again quit; this time for good, and joined the AA. During those dozen years, he would write in a series of revealing memoirs in the pages of *The Sunday Press*, how he had come to know 'hell on earth'.

He had more than once felt suicidal.

He lost all his money.

His marriage was in grave difficulties.

'There were spells of being on the dry,' Rackard wrote in *The Sunday Press*. 'There were other spells of being on the bash. There were car crashes and wild binges. There were blackouts, which experts know are nearly always a certain sign of alcoholism. Once I went to a ball on a Friday and came to in the local pub on the following Tuesday morning, still in my dress suit.

'Gradually, from Sunday drinking, it became weekend drinking.' Rackard made his first hospital visit in 1965. 'The more I refused to face up to the day, the more I drank. The more I drank the worse my nerves and fears became, and the more I ducked back to alcohol.'

Rackard admitted to being 'practically down and out' when he stopped drinking once and for all in his mid-40s. He said that he did not have enough money to buy a new set of tyres for his car, but from that point he rebuilt his life, rebuilt his veterinary practice, and got back into the game of hurling with a passion, in addition to also unleashing his passion for horses.

Rackard was travelling the country helping others with their afflictions when, in February of 1974, he noticed lumps on his neck that he had removed, but cancer had taken its hold. 'Some drinkers may not believe it but I know that sober, life is better,' he had written in *The Sunday Press*. 'The sky is bluer, and the perspectives sharper. And each morning I get up, I realize that this day is the first day of the rest of my life.'

Wexford had reached the semi-final of the league in 1976, despite losing by five points to Kilkenny in Enniscorthy in the final round of the competition. They would lose the semi-final replay to Clare, 4-16 to 3-24 after extra-time. Wexford lined out in Semple Stadium wearing black arm bands.

The Tricolour was at half mast in the ground.

I'd imagine most of us were there that morning... the morning they buried Nickey.

I remember it well... for the older fellas on the team, it was a poignant day because we'd all been involved with Nickey because he was a selector with us for a few years.

He was one of those... what would you call it... larger than life figures? A big man... I found him, I suppose... a gentleman no matter what way you looked at it, a big man as I said... but a quiet going fella, a humble fella.

Y'know, the type of fella that would have got on with nearly everyone. That's my memory of Nickey Rackard.

As regards hurling in Wexford, he was the King when I was growing up... he was everything to the likes of us... a leading light. He was one of three brothers of course playing for the county, and a part of a team that were all high profile figures because of their two All-Irelands and everything else they did, but still... Nickey Rackard stood out as someone above them all.

He might not have been the most vocal, I'd say... he wasn't a man who would take over in a dressing-room or anything like that... I suppose he didn't need to!

He was Nickey Rackard!

He could just, more or less, work away quietly in the background. That was how he operated.

At the time he was involved with the county, when I was playing and he was a selector... I suppose it might have been at the height of his problems.

It would have been, I'd say.

He had been more or less reforming before he pulled out of the GAA scene really.

He was strong enough to turn his life around... there would have been a lot of times in that period when he was quite normal... you could not say he was that way all of the time.

For most of the time that I knew him anyway, Nickey Rackard was as normal as any other person who didn't drink.

At the beginning of the summer of 1976, Tony Doran was amongst the greatest hurlers in the country who set off for a tour of the United States, and games on the east and west coasts – three in total against reigning All-Ireland champions, Kilkenny. At Notre Dame Stadium in Los Angeles, which was 120 yards long and only 70 yards wide and much too tight to even accommodate a 13-a-side game, the Allstars defeated Kilkenny by 4-13 to 2-18, a single point win, but a contest that everyone on the field was delighted to see end in the 85 degree heat.

There were over 5,000 people at the game, and hurling fans turned out in big numbers at Gaelic Park in New York too by the end of the month, over 7,000 people watching the Stars win by nine points, their third win on the trot.

In New York, Tony Doran battled it out with Brian Cody at full-back and Frank Cummins at centre-back, so it wasn't all fun and games for the tourists. But Doran scored his customary brace of goals to help entertain the locals.

Tony Doran was a 'replacement' on the tour in '76 but he would return the following summer having received his first and only Allstar award during the winter in between.

I don't remember an awful lot about those games, but the heat was unreal.

They'd start off and they would not be really competitive at all, but y'know... something might happen and, after that... they'd get competitive fairly quickly. One little thing... and they could take off at times.

New York at that time was the biggest attraction because it was closer to the largest Irish communities and the GAA scene in the States. New York and Boston as well, they were a bit like playing games at home, whereas Los Angeles was different.

We stayed with local families when we were out west, and that was fine, they were always very hospitable and they had fine big homes, but in New York we were always put up in hotels.

The only real problem for me on any of those trips was being up in the air. I was not a great traveller... I don't like flying.

I went... but each time I was never that happy with the travel end of things. I just had to make do with it. I recall, on one of the internal flights between two of the cities... between Los Angeles and San Francisco or vice-versa... there was a bit of a problem with the plane.

We were coming down... fairly close to landing... and air hostesses and everyone were getting into their seats and buckling up, and we looked out through the window... wasn't there a row of ambulances and fire brigades... either side of the runway!

One of the landing wheels or something was not coming down... but the pilot brought it down anyway.

There were sparks flying as he hit the ground.

We got there anyhow. They were prepared for the worst... when you look out and see what is lined up along either side of the runway... you'd be worried. But I didn't like flying even before that happened.

I was never a fan of flying, and even to the present time I'm no fan. I've gone back to the States since just the once, and I've been to London a good few times, but no matter how often I get up there I'm in a bit of a hurry to get my feet back down on the ground.

On June 14, Wexford got their championship campaign up and running in Athy. It was a Leinster semi-final, as Kildare had already accounted for Dublin in the first round and had the reward of hosting Doran and Co. Included in the Wexford starting line-up, making his championship debut between the sticks, was Buffers Alley teammate Henry Butler.

Wexford lost Teddy O'Connor and Willie Murphy from their full-back line before the game, and in a makeshift defence Butler faced greater pressure than any had expected. In the first-half alone he had to make three saves from Kildare full-forward, Michael Moore that were termed 'magnificent' in the pages of the *The Irish Press*. But Butler was not named the hero of the hour.

That title fell to another Wexfordman, Johnny Walsh – except he was wearing all white in Athy that same afternoon and playing right half-forward for the home team.

Living in Kill, Walsh had thrown in his lot with Kildare, and proceeded to demonstrate remarkable accuracy from a variety of angles for a personal contribution of 12 points on the day, six of them from play.

Wexford, at the other end during the first-half, had shot a dozen wides and found themselves 0-11 to 1-4 down at the change. It could have been much worse because, 21 minutes into that same half, Kildare led 0-9 to 0-2, with Johnny Walsh scoring eight of them. The other point came from the stick of

Walsh's brother, Ned.

Pat Dunny was looking unstoppable in the No.6 shirt for Kildare, and for the second-half the Wexford selectors brought Tony Doran out from the square. His job was to quieten down Dunny, and get things into motion on the scoring board.

That he did.

But a four points win, 2-19 to 2-15, did not send shivers down the spines of any Kilkenny hurlers listening in on their radios.

It was played in Athy, that game... and we were dead lucky to get out of it. It was only in the last 15 minutes or so that we really got the few scores to take over.

Henry was a good goalie... I can't say anything bad about him anyway, because he was a clubmate of mine! He was a good friend, and he was a very experienced goalie... a big man, six feet plus and had a great puck out.

He had a big day against Kildare, but he still lost his place for the Leinster final. John Nolan at the time was the regular and he came back for the game against Kilkenny.

Henry only got to play in one Leinster final. John was not in it for a couple of years and Henry had taken over in 1979, but John came back then again in the 80s. But Henry was a very, very good keeper. He had a long career with Buffers Alley and was our goalie for the best part of 30 years... he was still there in '89 when we won the All-Ireland club title.

He had started when we won the Intermediate Championship in '65... that was his first year playing in goal with the club and he played the whole way through... and after '89 he played for another couple of years.

Henry retired after that, but in '92 our goalie, Seamus Kavanagh broke his leg and Henry came back to play in a Leinster club final against St Rynagh's. He was playing junior at the time... he would have been about 44, I'd say... but he came back and had an outstanding game in the Leinster final.

No goals... and we won the Leinster title. He was a serious goalie over a long period, but the problem for Henry was that Nolan was a top class keeper as well.

I have to tell you this though... Henry was one of these fellas who did not like all the training, but still he lasted that long.

He wasn't a man for doing 10 or 20 laps.

That day against Kildare, Henry kept us alive... they were flying!

Johnny Walsh was doing most of the damage... and Johnny had played Intermediate with Wexford and won an All-Ireland in '61 when my brother, Bill was also a member of the winning team.

He was one of those who was talked of as a future Wexford inter-county star, and I don't know what happened or what went wrong... but he did not make the breakthrough and he moved to Kildare then to live and work. He played with Ardclough first... then he threw in his lot with Kildare. In some of those years he was picked as a replacement on some of the Allstar tours... and he was involved with Leinster on one or two years as well.

Walsh could do damage against any team.

He was a serious player... even at that stage in '76... when he was probably in his mid-30s.

It was 15 years since his Intermediate All-Ireland with Wexford... he must have been 34 or 35 years of age. Looking back, he certainly appears to have been one who slipped through the net as far as Wexford was concerned.

The championship of 1976 was a strange one for Wexford, and even more difficult for their supporters to work out.

The team's form was on some sort of mad roller-coaster.

They beat Kildare by four points, and in the All-Ireland semi-final against Galway they were lucky to take home a draw the first day, and only had one goal to spare over the Westerners in the replay.

Not the form of potential All-Ireland champions.

But, in between those matches against Kildare and Galway, something strange and wonderful occurred on July 18. In the Leinster final Wexford got to grips with defending provincial and All-Ireland champions, Kilkenny from the very beginning and, for once, Wexford never lost their grip.

They actually humbled the Cats.

They were six points up at half-time.

They finished the game with a 17 points advantage and a 2-20 to 1-6 scoreline.

'Where the hell did that come from?' Brian Cody wrote in his autobiography, *Cody*. 'One day, you're sailing merrily along without a wave in sight, not a single cloud in the sky and the weather forecast promising more of the same for the foreseeable future, the next you're shipwrecked on jagged rocks in the midst of a howling gale with all of your possessions scattered irretrievably.

'That's how it felt after the 1976 Leinster final which, according to popular opinion, was supposed to be a tricky but negotiable stepping stone for Kilkenny in our pursuit of the All-Ireland three in-a-row. Wexford hadn't beaten Kilkenny in the Leinster final for five years and, while there were some intense tussles in the interim – including a draw in 1972 – there was no reason to believe that Wexford would unseat us in 1976. Well none that we had spotted anyway.'

Kilkenny had been unbeaten in the championship since the 1973 All-Ireland final. And that defeat had been deemed 'unfortunate' by Cody and his teammates. The Cats could not have been any more confident as they had awaited Wexford in the '76 Leinster decider. They had beaten Clare in the league final replay – the teams had drawn in early May but had to wait for six weeks (due to the Allstars tour of the United States) before doing it all over again. Kilkenny won the second game easily, and perhaps they thought they could stroll through the Leinster campaign as well? Cody, playing at left corner-back, was at least saved from the full-on impact of Tony Doran who helped himself to one goal and two points, and created general mayhem for all of those around him in purple and gold to enjoy.

'Wexford didn't just beat us in the final – they demolished us and then steamrolled over the debris so that by the end of the day it was as if we never existed on a hurling field. From three in-a-row favourites to crushed non-entities and all in the space of one July afternoon in Croke Park.

'Wexford won by 2-20 to 1-6 which was, apparently, Kilkenny's biggest defeat in a Leinster final since the 1890s. To be honest, we were lucky to escape with a 17-points defeat. It said a lot about Wexford's superiority and our inept performance on the day that, only for a string of fine saves by Noel Skehan, we would have been thrashed by an even bigger margin. It sure is bad when you lose by 17 points and your goalkeeper is your best player.

'There was no obvious explanation as to why we were so off-tune that day. Fair play to Wexford, who produced a high-tempo performance, but even they would admit that we were incredibly poor. We would normally expect to score 1-6 in less than half an hour, yet that was our total return for 70 minutes.'

If Kilkenny thought they were going to gain revenge the following summer, they were wrong. In the 1977 Leinster final, in a much tighter and tougher affair altogether that produced six goals in total, Wexford came out on top by three points.

Cody took that defeat on the chin. 'In fairness to Wexford, they proved they had a very good team at the time,' he remembered. 'This time (1977) only a few points separated us, but it was more than enough to complete the Leinster final double over Kilkenny, something they hadn't done since the 1950s.'

It was one of those unreal days when everything clicked for us.

A Leinster final against Kilkenny was always going to have us as outsiders, and Clare had beaten us in the league semi-final replay so we had our heads down for a week or so after that. They then played a draw with Kilkenny in the league final, and the Allstar tour was in the middle of it, but then when Kilkenny came back home they beat Clare by 12 or 15 points in the league final replay.

It was just going to be a matter of form as far as everyone was concerned, business as usual for Kilkenny.

But in the Wexford group we did not look at it that way. We'd always been there or thereabouts with Kilkenny, every year... we felt that we were well capable of matching them again. As it happened, everything went perfect on the day.

John Quigley got a goal before half-time and then I got one shortly after in the second-half, and that effectively killed them off. With Kilkenny, of course, you could never be sure that they were dead... and properly buried.

But that was one day when I think Wexford kept going relentlessly, and we piled on the agony on them. They only scored one point in the second-half.

Hard to imagine?

Looking back now, I'd say to win by that much was a bit of a freak. There was no way we were 17 points better than Kilkenny. It was, I suppose, a little bit like a couple of occasions in the earlier part of the 70s when they beat us by more than 10 points in Leinster finals. Y'know, overall, it was not true to form either.

There was very little between the two teams for those five or six years, but there were occasional days when one team got a grip on the match. That's what happened in '76.

They took their beating well. We had taken it from them so often there was not much else they could do really. They were going for three in-a-row, and it must have been desperately disappointing... but there was no quibbles out of them.

In *The Irish Press*, Padraig Puirseal saw Tony Doran deposit the final nail in the Kilkenny coffin thus:

'Wexford virtually clinched the game five minutes after the restart when Doran, receiving from Christy Keogh, broke through to palm the ball to the Kilkenny net for a lead of 2-13 to 1-5. From that moment until the end the only question in doubt was the margin of Wexford's victory.

Doran played an inspiring part – a captain's part – in fashioning his team's success. Time and again he won possession in his duel with Nicky Orr, and Butler and John Murphy also thundered into the game to give their leader magnificent support.

Willie Rowsome stepped up his display at midfield to forge an unbeatable partnership with Jacob, while Teddy O'Connor was the equal of Doran as a figure of inspiration at right full-back. Colm Doran, at centre half-back, was in splendid form, too, and with Willie Murphy, Liam Bennett, Buggy and Prendergast, formed a defensive unit that Kilkenny could not breach. Goalkeeper John Nolan also played a distinguished part in the victory...'

Over-confidence was Wexford's biggest opponent in the All-Ireland semi-final against Galway on August 15. And definitely a more cunning and sinister opponent than the fifteen men who took the field in Pairc Ui Chaoimh in maroon.

However, the choice of venue was also a tricky hurdle to overcome.

Wexford were not happy having to travel to Cork. And some Wexford folk were far from thrilled that Frank Murphy, the secretary of the Cork County Board and a selector with the Cork team, who were awaiting their final opponents, was chosen as referee for the semi-final.

Martin Quigley looked to deal with the question of 'over-confidence' when asked his opinion by one newspaper man. 'There is, of course, a danger that our big win over Kilkenny will leave us in a complacent frame of mind,' he stated. 'But we have done and are still doing all we can to avoid that. In my time on the Wexford team I have never seen the players so keen, so eager, in preparation for a big game.' However, by even having to countenance the idea of the Wexford team battling with over-confidence, Quigley's words did show that Wexford had the idea far back in their minds that they might be lucky enough to have an easy step into the All-Ireland final.

'We can't let this opportunity pass,'Quigley stressed. 'We have a team not only capable of beating Galway but also of winning the All-Ireland final. I felt, and I think all the players were of the same impression, that we had a 50-50 chance of beating Kilkenny in the Leinster final. As you know, we won by 17 points, and that could very easily land us in a state of euphoria. I am certain, however, that we haven't let that happen...'

Galway had a preliminary championship win over Kerry by three points, but nobody was being entirely fooled by that slim victory. The last big meeting between the teams had been in Grace Park, in Athlone, six years before, but Galway were an entirely 'new' team, with only one member of that losing experience still playing – PJ Qualter, who had been right full-forward in Athlone, but was selected at full-forward for the 1976 All-Ireland semi-final (from where he would get in for two goals) in Pairc Ui Chaoimh.

Six Wexfordmen remained standing from that close encounter in Athlone: Teddy O'Connor, Martin and John Quigley, Mick Butler, Tony Doran and Mick Jacob. Two other members of the Wexford team, Willie Murphy and

Ned Buggy, had not been available for the game in 1970.

Pairc Ui Chaoimh was just newly refurbished and opened at the time... it was actually a very, very strange venue to bring Wexford and Galway to... playing down in Cork? From a travel point of view it was not the easiest place to get to... and it was very warm weather that summer.

I actually think those two semi-final meetings with Galway, the semi-final draw and then the replay... I think they lost the All-Ireland on us that year. I have always been firmly convinced of that ever since... and that's not me trying to take anything from Cork at the same time.

I am convinced that after the first day... when we could have won, but could have been beaten as well... we were in a spot of bother. Had we nicked it the first day, I still believe we would have had a much better chance of winning the All-Ireland.

It was a no-win situation for Frank Murphy, being appointed to referee the game against Galway... he was the secretary of the Cork County Board, he was a Cork team selector... I'd imagine no one really thought it through!

I can't remember us talking about it in our dressing-room. It wasn't an issue with us as players... it was just one of those things. I'd say on the first day no fault could be found with Frank's refereeing but, as I've said... he was in a no-win situation. People would think what they wanted to think!

The replay went on a week later... another sweltering warm day. It was such an open ground Pairc Ui Chaoimh... a bowl of a ground, and a bit of a sun trap!

Twice in seven days we had travelled to Cork and played in that ground and it took an awful lot out of the Wexford team... and we had only a two week gap to the All-Ireland final. With a team that was, I'd say... half of them on the wrong side of 30? I think it had a major effect on us... there were a lot of niggling injuries though most of them had cleared up before the final.

There was no problem with Frank Murphy refereeing the drawn game with Galway but Mick Slattery from Clare got the job of refereeing the replay instead of Murphy.

Sean Silke, Galway's strong-hearted centre-back, scored a late, late point to snatch a draw in the All-Ireland semi-final. He did so right at the death. Wexford had appeared to have done just enough. Two goals each from Mick Butler and Tony Doran and one from Ned Buggy seemed to have been sufficient as Wexford were holding on, 5-14 to 2-22. Before Silke boldly shot over his fourth point of the game.

Of course, Galway were now one of the powers of hurling, even if Wexford had a small dose of over-confidence to contend with before the drawn game.

Galway had won the National league in 1975 with a powerful 4-9 to 4-6 win over Tipperary, before losing to Kilkenny in the All-Ireland final. It was the eighth All-Ireland final the county had lost since claiming their first historic win in 1923. They had lost four in the 20s, and three more in the 50s, before going down again in '75.

But, there was a storm brewing in their maroon jersey – and one that the charismatic Cyril Farrell would perfectly control when he took over the management of the team in 1979, guiding the county to three famous All-Ireland titles in the 80s.

Back down in Pairc Ui Chaoimh, one week after the drawn semi-final, Wexford edged out a five-goal contest, 3-14 to 2-14, thereby holding onto their undefeated record against Galway in the championship, but only just. Wexford, once again, plundered goals – three of them in the first-half from Tony Doran, John Quigley and Ned Buggy to earn a 3-5 to 0-12 advantage.

Wexford edged the second-half by a single point, shooting over nine points to Galway's 2-2.

It was all too close for comfort.

And it was definitely sapping.

We got a great start in the All-Ireland final but we were not able to sustain it.

We definitely had problems in the last 15 minutes of that final against Cork... the two games against Galway came back to haunt us. Cork were fresher, they had no All-Ireland semi-final that year... Antrim were not in the senior championship and Cork were in great shape.

Maybe because of the lack of match practice they were that little bit slow to get going in the final, but when they got to the pace of it, they took off... and they had stronger legs than us down the home straight.

We had no manager, as such, in charge of us that year, if I remember... Tom Neville more or less was calling the shots... there was also Syl Barron, Mick O'Hanlon, Pat Murphy and Pat Nolan, our former goalkeeper... but I genuinely can't recall if any of them acted in the formal role of a manager!

Tom Neville... Tom was from O'Hanrahans in New Ross... he was more or less the one in charge, though Ned Power did most of the training still... assisted by Tom.

Paddy Downey recorded the game thus in the *The Irish Times* the following morning.

'With Tony Doran and the Quigley brothers leading the assault, Wexford made the best start any team could wish for in an All-Ireland final. After Butler (free) and Buggy had put up two points, Martin Quigley, waiting inside the Cork back line, turned Doran's pass to the net in the fifth minute. And he repeated the performance one minute later when he cracked the rebound home after Coleman had saved smartly from Doran.

That left Cork eight points in arrears and the game barely started. It was a daunting situation but with their midfielders totally dominant, they came to grips with it rapidly and after Moylan had opened their account in the ninth minute, scored a string of points which left them only one behind just after the turn of the first quarter.

Ray Cummins scored their first goal in the 30th minute when, losing his hurley, he raced through to kick the ball past John Nolan, and Cork then took the lead for the first time with points from O'Leary and McCarthy. But Wexford replied in kind and the scores were level at the break, 2-8 to 1-11.

Wexford's second-half onslaught began with a fine goal by Doran 55 seconds after the restart. John Murphy had joined Buggy at midfield in a switch with Billy Rowsome and this helped to break their rivals earlier stranglehold around the halfway line.

But of greater importance in the Leinster champions' resurgence was the magnificence of Jacob at centre-half. He caught the ball out of forests of hurleys, cleared mightily and at the same time covered up in other areas. With Colm Doran also superb at left half, Wexford had at last achieved the dominance they desired in the half-back line.

The attack benefited richly from the support and the Cork backs were frequently in direct trouble. Yet the Munster side's forwards were still battling on with grim resolution and the lead changed hands three times to keep the rival supporters in a state of agony.

Eventually, however, the Cork rearguard sealed off the dangerous loopholes, paving the way for the winning scores by Barry-Murphy, Cummins and Moylan.

Butler let slip a couple of good scoring chances for Wexford and their last hope vanished when the referee decided on a 'slap ball' as Wexford supporters roared in anticipation of a 21 yards free. Had that come, two minutes from full-time, the game could well have ended a draw...'

A 'slap ball' is not a term supporters ever come across in the modern game of hurling, but such a thing, a 'slap ball' caused consternation at the conclusion of the 1976 All-Ireland final.

The second-half of the game was in the lap of the Gods. And it began with Tony Doran collecting a John Quigley lob and rounding Pat McDonnell in the Cork goal with a side-step before shooting to the net.

A high ball came in from John Quigley and I caught it fairly close to the goal and finished it off.

They got a goal back quickly... it was a sort of see-saw in the second-half most of the time, and I think we were a couple of points up most of the time as well... and Cork then... they must have got about five points in the last 10 minutes.

And we didn't get a score.

Nothing.

I felt that the Cork mentors had been studying us well for those two games down in Pairc Ui Chaoimh, and they had everything fairly well worked out.

It's always been credited to Christy Ring that he was responsible for moving Jimmy Barry Murphy... in the switch that seemed to make the most impact. Jimmy was playing wing forward on Colm and he was getting no change there... and had hardly scored in 55 minutes, and they moved him in centre-forward on Mick Jacob.

It's always been said that Ring was the one who made the move because he saw Mick tiring. I would not want to condemn Mick Jocob over that... it's probably true that most of us were tiring... and overall Cork were fresher when it came to the home straight.

Jimmy Barry Murphy was only 22 years of age at the time... a young pup only, but he was a great athlete... with great pace.

Then there was a bit of controversy at the end of the game as well.

The game ended with Cork on a bit of a gallop.

In the 25th minute of the second-half Pat Moylan scored a point from a free to leave Cork just one point behind.

Two minutes later Jimmy Barry-Murphy levelled the scores.

Cork 2-17, Wexford 4-11.

One minute later Barry-Murphy put Cork in front by one.

Two minutes after that Ray Cummins kicked the sliotar over the bar.

One minute later, John Horgan cleared his lines with a mighty puck, and Barry-Murphy got on the end of it and shot another point.

Four minutes later, referee Paddy Johnston awarded a free to Cork, and Moylan slotted it over the bar.

Cork 2-21, Wexford 4-11.

Full-time.

A four points win for Cork, expertly timed no doubt about that at all, but it was the referee's decision to decide on a 'slap ball' that had most people talking in the temperamental, and agonising hours for Wexford, after the game.

They were mighty vexed with the referee.

And it did not help that the referee happened to be a Kilkenny man.

Though Paddy Johnston was a good and honest man, and someone who was rightly hailed as a fair and judicious controller of all games, someone who showed no fear, no favour whatsoever... he was still a Kilkenny man.

A high ball came in from out the field... just to the left of the Canal goal... just slightly to the Cusack Stand side... and I caught it.

Brian Murphy had been playing corner-back and had moved in full-back on me. I had been playing on Pat McDonnell to begin with.

Murphy had moved in... and I caught it on Brian and cut inside him... because, at that stage, there was nothing in my head... only to head for goal.

I felt he threw his arms around me and pulled me down to the ground.

The two of us were suddenly on the ground and everyone thought it was a 21-yards free... a free in to us!

But the referee came in and was slow to do it at first... and next thing, he decided to throw the ball in.

I don't know how he could have arrived at that decision... and more than likely I told him what I thought of it at the time as well... more than likely!

I know from talking to Brian Murphy umpteen times since... and being in his company when people are getting onto him... y'know... but Brian only smiles!

And that nearly says it all.

For me... anyhow.

At the luncheon for both teams the next day, Paddy Johnston's decision was still the talk of the town in Dublin. Before the senior and minor teams sat down to eat, there was a general invitation, as usual, to watch a re-run of RTE's videotape of the match in The Garda Club. Wexford people watching were doubly incensed. Cork folk suggested that Tony Doran may have been charging with the ball and that was why the referee made a decision to throw the ball in. 'It is impossible to be definite about what happened,' commented John Quigley. 'But I can't see how it could have been a slap ball. If it wasn't a free in for Wexford, then it should have been a free out for Cork.'

The Cork coach, Fr Bertie Troy was not getting into that argument, but instead was happy to talk about the move to switch Barry-Murphy. 'Because he had not been in many of the hard exchanges,' the good priest explained, '... we felt that he was fresh enough to face the Wexford centre half-back, Mick Jacob, who had played a great game and must have been tiring at that time. The move worked... Jimmy got the scores that won it for us. We used him in the same way as a substitute in the Munster semi-final against Tipperary.'

Frank Murphy also kept out of the heated debate. 'We had what looked like a disastrous start,' he considered. 'But the team didn't panic. They had been coached to face that sort of situation over several months.'

Cork supporters also commented that they were mightily relieved to see Mick Butler miss with a free they thought he would convert nine minutes from the end. Cork were two points behind at that stage, 4-11 to 2-15, and they felt that a three-points gap might have been a yawning one.

The Cork voices insisted that was the turning point, and not the 'slap ball', because the ball was cleared after Butler's miss and Cork won a free down the other end of the field, and Moylan popped over a point to make it a one-point game instead of a three-point game.

In *The Irish Press*, Padraig Puirseal, after having his bite to eat, reported thus:

'There was a conflict of opinion yesterday about the decision of referee Paddy Johnston to award a 'slap ball' – a throw-in between players of both sides – two minutes from the end of the All-Ireland hurling final between Cork and Wexford at Croke Park on Sunday.

After the match, a number of Wexford players and many of their supporters were furious about the decision. They claimed that Tony Doran was fouled by the Cork back, Brian Murphy, and that a free in should have been awarded on the 21-yards line, almost directly in front of goal. With Cork three points in front at the time, that would have given the Leinster champions a chance of drawing the game. Ned Buggy, they said, would have had a 50-50 chance of scoring a goal...'

The luncheon for the two teams was always an awkward meeting. Wexford, naturally, would have preferred to head straight back home, but for Cork, with Liam MacCarthy on show, and the added bonus of a trip to the United States on the Allstars tour the following spring, there were no worries at all about spending another long day in Dublin before finally getting home and celebrating with their own.

Though, when the 1976 Allstar team was announced on October 19, it told the story in explicit detail of Wexford's strength right through the championship. There were four wexfordmen named, one less than Cork.

But the four of them – Willie Murphy, Mick Jacob, Martin Quigley and Tony Doran – won the No.3, No.6, No.11 and No. 14 jerseys on the Allstar team, forming a powerful spine.

Tony Doran would be named team captain.

Awful, awful things... those lunches, if you were the losing team.

They did not show the match during the lunch itself, which was something to be grateful for, I suppose... but previously, in past years, they had shown the match when the two teams sat down to eat.

I remember being at it in '70 when Cork beat us and beat us out the gate and they showed the match that day... and Christ, it was the same as if you were still in Croke Park with the shouting and the cheering... from the Cork people that were there. I think there was very, very little socialising.

They didn't mean any harm. They were still on a high and in the middle of their celebrations. But for us, what could you do?

You went through the motions of it, but you stuck with your own and tried to get through the day as best you could do.

Only Corkman I can remember talking to was Christy Ring... that Monday in 1976.

He was one of their selectors. He came over to me and sat down beside me, and I had no clue what he was wanting to talk about?

It turned out he did not want to talk about the All-Ireland at all... he wanted to arrange a challenge match for the following weekend with Glen Rovers and the Alley.

That was Ring's only worry that day... he was ready to move onto the next match. And the Glen and Christy Ring came up to our place for the game the following week.

That was the only thing in Ring's head... not a word to me about the All-Ireland at all.

Sure, even then he had a giant presence... he was a living legend... but it was strictly business in our conversation.

Those two or three days after the All-Ireland are the hardest, but the hardest of all is the Monday morning... when you wake up.

Like most people, I always think there are several All-Irelands maybe we left behind us, but that game in '76... definitely... it was one that we could have won... we definitely could have won it.

But when you wake up on the Monday morning... first thing is, you get a fright... and then you wonder... you wonder are you dreaming? And then the memory of the match hits you... hits you like a train.

That first hour, and the cold sweats you'd have with the memory of the game.

It's awful.

That was my feeling after big games, nearly always... but losing the All-Ireland there is a whole year gone in your life.

You are not normal for days after it... surely not... and Tuesday morning is just as bad... takes three or four days to get it out of your system and it does not leave your system until you get back playing another match.

That was the only way for me, anyway, to get over a loss of that magnitude... the only way to get over something like that and get it out of your system.

You had to get back out on the field.

Find your feet again, I suppose?

Even if you worked as hard as you could on the farm in the days afterwards, you'd still not be able to forget about the game... for those few days.

You'd go through the motions... do what had to be done, and... listen to all of the inquests from everyone around the area... and wait for the days to pass as fast as they could.

I don't know whether it is harder, or easier, getting through a disappointment like that... and not taking a drink.

You are on your own if you are not drinking... on your own within the group really.

Other lads might wish to drink through it all for a couple of days, and maybe the intensity of the disappointment is still waiting for them when they stop drinking... but, for me, as someone who didn't take a drink, you do feel you are on your own... and it is very, very tough.

Never crossed my mind to join them... and have a drink... never, never.

Like everyone else, I didn't want to go to bed at all on the night of the All-Ireland final... after any All-Ireland final defeat.

That's the last thing you want to do... you do not feel like going to bed... because, well... you know full well the horror that's awaiting you the next morning.

It would not be in my head to go to bed at all after a day like that.

Chapter 9

When the All stars team and All-Ireland champions, Cork reached the west coast of the United States in May of 1977 they were welcomed by Mary Foley, who quickly turned heads. *'Tall, willowy and strikingly feminine,'* one newspaper man informed his readers upon first meeting Mrs Foley.

The mother of five grown-up children was the tour's hostess, and was on hand to see to it that Allstars manager, Jim Berry from Wexford, and Allstars captain Tony Doran and his fellow players, were quickly made to feel at home, though Mary Foley was a busy woman. In addition to acting as the president of the Irish Games Committee in Los Angeles, she was also one of the top executives in the leading Irish-American travel agency in the city and also found time to study sociology at Glendale City College.

The Irish media pack – another suggested Mrs Foley would have *'been more at home in a modeling role'* – was won over.

'I have to confess that I was a little apprehensive last October when I was invited to go forward for the presidency,' Mary explained to them, further informing them that she (and some others who resented a woman taking charge of GAA affairs), wondered if she could fill the shoes of her predecessor Pat Daly, who had retired from his role in charge of welcoming the Irish teams. She also had to calm things between the Irish communities in her native city and San Francisco. A feud was simmering between the pair of cities.

The United Irish Societies in San Francisco – which sounds like a pretty forceful body, does it not? – were still in a huff over losing out on the 'opening Sunday' to Los Angeles the previous year.

Mary, of course, solved it all. She got in touch with the president of the United Societies, JJ Whelan and 'hopped on the next plane', and the two cities were bosom buddies by the time Berry, Doran and Co landed on the west coast. Though Mary had managed to talk JJ into giving LA the first Sunday once again!

'For the first time, I think we may come out with a little profit,' Mary revealed, adding that her committee was contributing $12,000 towards the cost of the tour. 'And we can go forward immediately with our plans to make the games in Los Angeles better than ever next year.'

On the field of play, Cork had won the opening encounter with the Stars back in Chicago, 5-7 to 3-10, but in the Notre Dame High School Stadium in Los Angeles, Doran's men turned the tables with a resounding 2-15 to 1-7 victory, a Doran goal coming seven minutes into the second-half to give his team a commanding 1-10 to 0-3 advantage. PJ Molloy from Galway added the second goal in front of a decent crowd of approximately 5,000 people. Not all of the tour party made it to the game, however, as a visit to the Disneyland theme park was heard being discussed by some, and others had a fancy for heading to Hollywood Park for some racing.

'Come here, I can see hurling any Sunday at home,' one Corkman, who remained nameless told *The Irish Press*.

'… but there's no Disneyland near Patrick Street!'

The third and decisive game of the tour, at Balboa Stadium in San Francisco, was a bit of a thriller indeed, and a goal from Tony Doran two minutes before half-time got the Stars back into it and reduced the deficit to 1-9 to 1-6. But Cork, who had squeezed in two sneaky training sessions after their defeat in LA, pushed hard on the resumption and won 2-17 to 1-15.

The league campaign before Christmas had not seen Wexford coming out of the blocks with all guns blazing, and in the three games played at the tail end of 1976 there were three quick defeats on the trot, losing by one point to Tipperary in Clonmel, losing by five to Kilkenny in Nowlan Park, and by seven to Clare in New Ross. A first win came against Dublin in Gorey (2-17 to 1-7).

When the league resumed after the Christmas break there was a draw with Limerick and a four points loss to Offaly. There were also two games against Cork in the spring of 1977. On February 2, in the Gold Model senior hurling final at Wexford Park, it looked like the home team had done enough but a Martin Doherty goal and a point from Pat Moylan at the death denied them (2-12 to 0-15), but a couple of weeks later, in the same neck of the woods, Wexford enjoyed a one point victory (2-15 to 4-8) over the Rebel County.

Before the start of the championship in '77, Tony Doran had indeed seen more than enough of Cork. Five times in total.

But they would see one another soon enough again.

Beating Cork in the league got us back on track for the rest of the year. It was an important win... we hadn't been really on top of things up until then.

Some times, after a tough loss like the one we had in the All-Ireland final, a team is left with a bit of a... hangover, I suppose you might call it. Beating Cork by that one point in the league cleared our heads.

We did not mix with the Cork lads that much when we were in America. We had nothing against them, of course... but it was different to Kilkenny because, well... we knew the Kilkenny lads an awful lot better.

Cork kept to themselves more... but there were no problems with them! That tour to America was more famous for bad blood between the footballers from Dublin and Kerry... oh yeah, there was skin and hair flying between them.

In the press box, the gentleman with their pens in the front row, were of the opinion that Kilkenny, after giving so much in the 70s, and winning their fair share, were close to a busted flush, though the Cats had fought well during the league and managed to reach the final.

There they went under to Clare by five points, however, and even though Kilkenny surely had revenge on their minds (for the battering they had received 12 months earlier) Wexford were everyone's favourites when Leinster's big two once again met in the Leinster final on July 24.

It should not have been a cliffhanger, but it turned out exactly like that (3-17 to 3-14), as John D Hickey in *The Irish Independent* reported:

'The only question left unanswered at the end was how it was that Kilkenny were in the match until the last puck and might have won it were it not for two crucial saves by John Nolan in the middle of the second-half.

Nolan needed those two saves to redeem himself for a dreadful error before the match was five minutes old but he never allowed it to unsettle him and could afford a flamboyant excursion from his goal in the second-half to prove that his confidence was as soundly based as ever.

Some of the wiseacres were nodding their heads and talking of an end of an era in Kilkenny hurling as the black and amber-shirted players trooped to their dressing-room at the end with the whooping of the jubilant Wexford throngs ringing in their ears. In truth it is difficult not to see the result in other than these stark terms. There were clear signs of lack of mobility in some of the more senior Kilkennymen. Eddie Keher has not had as quiet a day for many a year; Kieran Purcell never showed any sign of his devastating score-grabbing; Pat Henderson was a clear loser in his battle with Tony Doran and Matt Ruth seldom sparkled as he can.

That is not to suggest that any or all of these men should consider applying for the old-age pension or a grant to provide themselves with a wheelchair but, when the exchanges were at their most furious and when spirit and muscle were being tested, it seemed that the Wexfordmen came out of the test with their reputations intact and with the ball in their grasp.

But it is to Tony Doran that most of the credit must go for this splendid Wexford achievement. There is the hallmark of the skilled craftsman rather than the signature of the grand master on all his work. He is happiest where there is least space and seems to relish the hot breath of his pursuers on the nape of his neck. His two goals were sweetly taken – both with the palm – and if he missed the hat-trick he will surely claim that it was a mistaken decision by officials which robbed him of it rather than any lack of effort on his part.'

We were well on top generally in that Leinster final, and I think... well, we did let them back at us a bit in the last 10 minutes.

It was a good, convincing win... even if it never looked like it on the scoreboard. We never looked like losing it.

Brian Cody got a goal for them near the start, from a '70'... somehow the ball ended up in the back of the net.

It was a strange one. I scored my two goals that day with the hand... which I know some people never liked that much, but a goal is a goal... and that was allowed back then.

At that time, the way hurling was played... unlike now... it was right for fellas to be able to score with the hand. It suited the game at that time... for one thing it brought more goalmouth action into it... and it brought more goals into games and helped to make them more exciting.

Wexford were back in the All-Ireland final.

And Cork were on their way to meet them in Croke Park on September 4. Two Seanie O'Leary goals were just enough to see them through against Waterford (4-13 to 3-11) in the Munster semi-final, and two more from Jimmy Barry-Murphy were crucial in another five points win (4-15 to 4-10) in the provincial final against Clare. They had yet another five-points win in the All-Ireland semi-final, 3-14 to 1-15 against Galway. Cork were plundering and piling the goals high all through the summer of '77, but in Christy Ring's head Cork needed to stop Tony Doran scoring goals if they were to successfully defend their All-Ireland title.

'Cork are champions and that could be a problem for Wexford, the challenging team are often over-anxious,' stated Ring, who was still a member of Cork's five-man selection committee. 'They will be very keen to beat us of course, because of last year's result.

'Wexford will have gained a lot of confidence from beating Kilkenny twice, it will give them a big uplift. Very few teams, at any time, would have done that.

'Tony Doran is their trump card.

'He is a great player and he can take the knocks,' stressed Ring. 'We must hold Doran at all costs.'

And the Cork defence did hold Tony Doran – for 20 minutes!

As in the previous year's decider, Mick Butler opened the scoring, receiving the ball from Ned Buggy and firing over after just 15 seconds.

Charlie McCarthy, Jimmy Barry-Murphy and Gerald McCarthy each replied for the holders, before John Quigley got Wexford's second. It was 0-3 to 0-2 after 10 minutes, and another thriller appeared on the cards for the attendance of 63,168, which was 500 fewer than watched the 1976 final for some reason.

But Cork, unlike '76, when they took their time getting into the match, continued to keep their noses in front, out-scoring Wexford by four points (including a magnificent Tom Cashman sideline from 50 yards out, and a Seanie O'Leary special after he twisted and turned Teddy O'Connor before striking on the turn) to one (Ned Buggy striking a 68-yards free) in the second 10 minutes of the match.

It was 0-7 to 0-3, when Doran struck.

The first goal of the day had its beginnings on the Wexford 50 yards line where Seanie O'Leary was penalised for dropping his hurley in passing. Mick Jacob drifted the resultant free towards the Cork goalmouth. Martin Doherty failed to deal with the danger, managing to only pat the ball down to John Crowley, who failed to come to grips with the situation.

Doran pounced, and whipped the ball first time to the net. Colm Doran then placed Butler for the equalising point.

At the other end, Ray Cummins laid the ball off beautifully for Gerald McCarthy to retake the lead on 30 minutes, and a full five minutes later Charlie McCarthy pointed a free to leave Cork 0-9 to 1-4 in front at half-time.

But Cork looked the better team.

And Wexford needed to reappear for the second-half, a changed and recharged fifteen, but that didn't happen and although Buggy opened the scoring when the game recommenced, Cork never looked over their shoulder, not even 13 minutes in when Buggy scored Wexford's second goal from a free after Tony Doran was fouled.

Wexford looked second best the entire second-half, and by the time Cork took their last score of the day in the 22nd minute of the half the champions were eight points in front (1-17 to 2-6).

With eight minutes left on the clock, Mick Butler pulled on the ball in a packed goalmouth and scored a third goal for Wexford. One minute later, Buggy tagged on a point from a free, but there was no big finish from Wexford.

They didn't score again for three minutes, when Buggy shot over a free from 60 yards, and they didn't score again over the last four minutes of the game.

Cork 1-17, Wexford 3-8.

It was an All-Ireland final that did not quite live up to its billing but, like '76, it did leave another controversial incident in its wake – and one involving Seanie O'Leary and his 'lost' hurley that left Wexford supporters more frustrated than furious. They knew in their hearts the better team had won.

Lost stick or no lost stick!

And in the pages of *The Irish Press*, Padraig Puirseal described it thus:

'... Fighting back from arrears of eight points (1-17 to 2-6), the challengers almost forced a draw three minutes from full time when a great shot from Christy Keogh was saved from point blank range by the Cork goalkeeper Martin Coleman.

To prove his class, Coleman stopped another rasper from John Quigley, but that effort was unnecessary, for the whistle had sounded for a free puck several seconds before the ball left the forward's hurley.

Wexford would not have deserved a replay. Cork, clearly in command at midfield all through the game, and showing a greater depth of hurling skill in every line, would not have been flattered had they won by nine or 10 points, instead of a vulnerable three.

But had they been held to a draw the champions could have blamed only themselves for wasting numerous scoring chances. They struck the ball wide from long range 10 times in the second-half for a total of 16 misses over the 70 minutes (Wexford's relative figures were six and two) and Jimmy Barry Murphy and substitute Tadgh Murphy each let slip excellent chances of goals.

Strangely, the winners failed to score in the last 13 minutes. It was in that period that Wexford played with real determination for the first time. A goal by Mick Butler, who shipped the ball through a forest of legs and hurleys after the Cork defence smothered Ned Buggy's low drive from a free at the Canal End, triggered a fierce offensive in the last few minutes, but the champions held on and undoubtedly deserved to survive.

'... Compared to the team that lost to the same opposition in a great final a year ago, Wexford were a poor side. The attack relied too heavily on Tony Doran, and with the full-forward effectively marked by the Cork full-back, Martin O'Doherty, the cutting edge of the front division was badly blunted.'

It was cruel to lose to them again but, it was a final defeat that we could have no complaints about... three points in it at the very end... and I suppose we could have nicked it at the end as well, but Cork were the far better team on the day.

We were the better team in '76... but Cork were far better in '77.

The game wasn't as open as the previous year. Cork were the more clinical team in everything they did... and then of course they got a controversial goal that also helped them.

It used to be that you could drop the hurley and palm the ball to the net, but that rule was changed... and instead you'd have to have the hurley in your hand... you could not drop it and palm the ball to the net.

Seanie O'Leary got the Cork goal midway through the second-half and Seanie seemed to have dropped the hurl before he palmed the ball home... it was the only goal Cork got, and all of the Wexford backs around him swear to this day that he dropped the stick and palmed it to the net... but... the goal stood.

As it was we could have nicked it in the end... Martin Coleman made a great save from Christy Keogh about a minute or two from the end for what would have been an equaliser. It could have changed it.

We were on a roll at the time and it was a little bit like the previous year, when Cork were on top of us in the last 10 minutes... except, this time in '77, we were all over them when it mattered at the end of the game, but we couldn't get the scores we needed.

If you dropped the hurl anywhere on the field it was a free. It was up to the referee's discretion... he had to decide if you dropped it on purpose, or if it was pulled out of your hand?

With that Seanie O'Leary goal... the ref said the hurley was pulled from his hand, but all of the Wexford backs swore... 'NO WAY'.

It was a very controversial rule at the time. It had come in that year, right at the start of '77.

I don't know why it came in?

A lot of them used to say that I was palming too many goals, but I dunno... I'd say I was getting a few that way alright, but everyone else was getting them that way as well.

Ray Cummins would have got quite a few at the time with his hand. Forwards in every county would have used their hands more to finish off scores... and, I suppose, some people looked at it and thought that it wasn't hurling really.

So, the rule came in... and it said that if you held onto your hurl then you could palm away. But, if you dropped your hurl, you couldn't!

The rule said that if you dropped the hurl anywhere on the field, and palmed the ball, it was a free. For a long time players forgot and still did it.

It was a controversial rule and it didn't make that much sense to me... but in that All-Ireland final itself we got on top of Cork in the last 10 minutes... got on a roll, and we were after scoring a goal and a few points.

Christy Keogh was clean through and let fly for the top corner and Coleman made his save... an amazing save... Martin Coleman got his hurley to it and deflected it out to the side, but nine times out of 10 it would have been in the net.

If it went in and if we had levelled it, then... to be honest, if anyone was going to win the game it would have been Wexford at that stage... we had taken complete control.

We got no momentum in the final at all until that last 10 minutes... we were very sluggish throughout the first-half and I still can't put my finger on it... or understand why?

There were enough post-mortems afterwards... in the days and weeks after the game... two years in-a-row we'd lost to Cork... there was a lot of talking about what happened... but talking doesn't change the result.

Chapter 10

The thought that Kilkenny were dead, and might be buried for some time, was soon to look entirely ridiculous.

Kilkenny would win the All-Ireland title again in 1979, and again in 1982 and '83 – and again and again, in 1992 and '93, and while Liam Griffin would lead Wexford the whole glorious way in 1996, Kilkenny would announce their old full-back Brian Cody as their new manager two years after that. And another 11 All-Ireland titles would follow in Cody's amazing era, without Wexford ever getting another look-in on the biggest stage of all.

In the final seasons of Tony Doran's career in the purple and gold, Kilkenny already had new blood flowing through the black and amber.

Paddy Prendergast from Clara, a product of St Kieran's College also – and who won Leinster and All-Ireland minor medals at No.3 for the Cats in 1975 – would play in five All-Ireland senior finals between 1978 and '87, and man the prized full-back position in their All-Ireland victory in '79.

Prendergast, not the most flamboyant of full-backs, would prove the durability and dependability of the conveyor belt serving Kilkenny. He did not make his championship debut at right corner-back until the county's 1978 Leinster semi-final win over Offaly, but headed home with his first Leinster medal a few weeks after that when Kilkenny accounted for Wexford. In the All-Ireland final Kilkenny lost out to a late goal from Cork which swung the match in their direction.

But, in the course of Kilkenny's victory over Wexford in the 1979 Leinster final, Prendergast was switched from the corner to full-back. He held onto the post for the All-Ireland final against Galway; the westerners having stopped Cork in the tracks towards a four in-a-row. Kilkenny would win by seven points. Prendergast never looked back.

After that, of course, the Kilkenny No.3 shirt was in the possession of Brian Cody in 1982 and '83. A man who would win colleges, minor, under-21, senior and club All-Ireland titles, before embarking on his stellar career as a manager and becoming the most successful team boss in the history of the GAA. Anyone wondering how Kilkenny came about so many incredibly talented and ambitious men in their defence, needs to look no farther than Cody's early, formative years.

He learned his trade.

Usually, the hardest way in Kilkenny! Cody was centre-back, in 1973, in one of the most incredible county finals ever played in Nowlan Park. At one point in the first-half James Stephens led by 13 points against The Fenians, and at half-time they still held onto a 10 points advantage, but a Fenians' comeback inspired by Pat Henderson, Pat Delaney and Nicky Orr finished with a 7-8 to 5-10 victory.

That was Kilkenny hurling, true and true.

Cody, however, had more to learn. He made his championship debut at No.3 for Kilkenny in the 1980 Leinster semi-final win over Wexford, but that same summer his proud and lofty ambitions were smashed over the head in the provincial final by Offaly, who won their first Leinster title by 3-17 to 5-10.

Cody started the Leinster semi-final against Wexford in 1981 on the substitutes bench – but when the new-look defence began to wobble he was quickly called into action. The following year Brian Cody was full-back.

And he held the position as Kilkenny claimed the Liam MacCarthy Cup in 1982 and defended it in '83.

The Wexford team of 1978, however, did not give up without a mighty fight against Kilkenny. In the league campaign they overcame Kilkenny by one point (1-11 to 2-7), in Wexford Park in November, and they fought it out against Kilkenny in the league semi-final in Dr Cullen Park in Carlow in April. The teams drew, 2-8 to 3-5, and the replay seven days later was of epic quality, Wexford losing by one point on a phenomenal scoreline of 5-15 to 5-14.

In 1978 we had those two big games against Kilkenny early in the year, and then when we both got to the Leinster final there was nothing between the teams yet again... we just knew one another so well... every trick, every strength... we were well matched.

That Leinster final... we lost by a goal... imagine!

We'd played one another four times that season, and all that separated us over the four games was a single goal.

It was fairly touch and go the whole time between us.. right to the very end of the 70s.

But... same old story.

In *The Irish Press*, Peadar O'Brien tried his damndest to bring home the thrilling nature of 1978 Leinster final for his readers.

'When all other matters have been taken into account and weighted against each other in the balance, there is only one thing left to decide the outcome of matches between two equally well-equipped teams. That one other thing is the lucky bounce or the unlucky slip and so it was between Kilkenny and Wexford at Croke Park yesterday, when Wexford's two-year reign as Leinster champions was ended in as tense and exciting a game of hurling as any would wish to see.

In this case, what became between Wexford and a possible victory, or at least an opportunity to try conclusions another day, was the thickness of the left-hand upright at the Canal End of the ground. Kilkenny were leading by two points at the time and there were about ten minutes left in the match. Christy Keogh grabbed the ball deep in his own half of the field and cleared it mightily down the field. As Tony Doran, Phil Larkin and others fought a torrid battle beneath the dropping ball John Quigley ran behind them and, as luck would have it, found the ball knocked down to him as he ran. He adjusted his stride a fraction and, without daring to look for Noel Skehan in the Kilkenny goal, he swung with all his might.

Skehan was in two minds and could not have been blamed had the ball entered the net, but Quigley's shot was pulled that fraction too finely and the ball struck the upright and came back into play to gasps of relief and chagrin from the rival supporters...'

Wexford, surprising nobody, refused to lose heart by that incident. They fought on grimly and were on level terms. They then edged their way into the lead, but were dealt another blow to the solar plexus. Matt Ruth scored a goal against the run of play at the other end.

O'Brien continued:

'It was enough to break even the staunchest hearts and after Kilkenny had scored two more points to give them a four-point lead it was clear that Wexford's great run of supremacy in Leinster was over.

But if Wexford go home with a feeling that the fates have been unkind to them once again, they can at least take great pride in the fact that they contributed to a marvellous contest. Skill, fitness and courage were all there in plenty for a crowd of more than 30,000.

Many memorable things remain in the mind. Frank Cummins scored an early point for Kilkenny when he doubled inside a tackle and swept the ball over the bar with his heels still on the sideline under the Cusack Stand. Eddie Walsh made some streaking runs through flailing hurleys, after coming on for John Quigley who had to go off on a stretcher with a split scalp.

Matt Ruth did some unselfish running and working for his colleagues. Billy Fitzpatrick wriggled and juggled and then scored the point of the match in the second half. Dick O'Hara was immaculate.

For Wexford, Tony Doran made a number of spectacular catches. Ned Buggy was in deadly scoring form from frees and play. Dave Bernie scored a point with a splendidly struck sideline cut. John Nolan made at least one memorable save and Martin Quigley looked everywhere for opportunities to advance his team's cause.'

But Wexford lost the 1978 Leinster final.

Kilkenny 2-16, Wexford 1-16.

Wexford lost, and in the process, incredibly, Paddy Prendergast, Fan

Larkin and Dick O'Hara, usually combined in the full-back line, held Tony
Doran scoreless.

Hard to imagine... the three of them managing that.

In 1979, the two teams met once again, in Nowlan Park in April in the
National league and, once more, they were virtually inseparable. It ended
1-10 to 1-9 in Kilkenny's favour, and brought a disappointing league to an
end for Wexford, and one that saw them relegated from the top division. The
pair, however, were destined to fight it out in one more – and the very last –
Leinster final of the decade.

Though Wexford barely made it through to the decider, finding Offaly
a handful in the provincial semi-final and only managing to win their way
through by the slimmest of margins, 0-17 to 2-10.

*That Leinster semi-final in '79 against Offaly was the only
Championship match I ever missed with Wexford.*

*I got my finger broken in a tournament game against Galway
shortly before it. I was back for the Leinster final... just barely
back playing again, and I did my bit in a Leinster final that could
have gone either way.*

I had a bandage on the finger but it was fine.

*Strange thing about those meetings between ourselves and
Kilkenny, the crowds were never huge... not compared to what you
see nowadays anyway.*

*Whether it was the fact of the two teams meeting so often in
Leinster finals, I don't know... but mid-20s in attendance was the
normal thing then. That was the general size of the crowd those
years in the final... small... even though there were no games on
telly at the time.*

*It was funny... you would always meet people who were not at
the games... and they'd ask you so many questions about what
happened up in Croke Park. But, I suppose, about that time it
wasn't as popular going to big matches as it is today.*

*Usually, the ground was not half full... mostly the genuine
followers went, people who went the whole time.*

Whereas today, when it comes to big days... you get a lot of people who would not be regular match-goers and... on top of that, there's a bigger fanfare in the media and on television about every single game, and far more noise than there ever was in our day.

The marketing and exposure to greater numbers of people now is huge... it makes it more attractive, and tells people that Croke Park is where they should be.

In our day, a game would be mentioned in the papers, but that was it.

An awful lot of people who go to matches today would not have gone to matches in the 70s.

The officials housed in Croke Park had invested in an electronic scoreboard by the very end of the 70s, thereby ending the days in which spectators, and players as well, would have to squint at the boards over either the Canal or Railway end of the ground.

The scoreboard was on the Hill end at the beginning... and then they had one on the Canal End. I remember the old scoreboard was on the back of the Hill sort of... before there was only one on the Canal End... and it would have goals and points.

When they put one up on the Canal End it gave the aggregate score of points only... which was a help.

As players you would always be keeping a check on it, especially in a tight match... you'd be doing the maths to see where you stood. At the time it was an old black board, and small enough and not distinguishable. You'd be wondering... 'Where are we?'

The electronic board was huge, however, and it made it easier to see... it was a help, and you didn't have to look hard at the other boards anymore.

We had the winning of that Leinster final in '79, we definitely had. But, while it was a game we could have won, we didn't manage to finish it off and... to be honest, after that defeat, it looked a little bit like Kilkenny were back in charge of affairs in Leinster.

That was Tony Doran's last Leinster final against Kilkenny.

He would play in two more, in the first half of the 1980s, but by then there was a third force at play in the province, and in 1981 and '84 Offaly stood tall – taller still because they were under the management of a Kilkennyman, Diarmuid Healy. Offaly, in fact, had a likeness of Kilkenny.

And, between them, Kilkenny and Offaly would see to it that Tony Doran would never win another Leinster title.

Kilkenny won the 1979 battle for the Leinster title by four points (2-21 to 2-17), at the end of another 'battle royal', but with an attendance of only 24,991 which was half of that that squeezed into Semple Stadium for the Munster decider between Cork and Limerick one week earlier.

Those who did not bother turning up missed a rip-roaring beginning, as in the first nine minutes of the game, Kilkenny and Wexford combined, scored more than the two Munster teams had managed in an entire first-half.

Leinster finals between Kilkenny and Wexford were becoming old hat to Paddy Downey, but he loved this one as much as any he had viewed before:

'... And the game went on, with point following point in rapid succession at either end and the electronic scoreboard flashing and blinking each change in the state of the parties, and overworked reporters might well have shouted, "Stop the Lights!"

Fifteen players contributed to the aggregate total – eight of them on the Kilkenny side. And the leading marksman for the winners was Mick Brennan, who shot eight marvellous points from play, often under extreme pressure, from the right corner. Ned Buggy, with 1-6, all from the dead ball, was top scorer of the day. His goal came from a penalty shot in the ninth minute and he sent the ball over the bar from a sideline cut 50 yards out to level the scores at 1-10 each, seconds before the half-time whistle.'

The scores had been level three times in that first-half. And the teams would be all-square four more times after they changed ends, though midway through the second-half a Wexford surge did appear to give them a firm control of proceedings. Wexford shot over three points, and then in the 44th minute Tony Doran turned the ball past Noel Skehan with an overhead stroke from Martin Casey's centre. Wexford were in front, 2-14 to 1-11.

Just as quick, however, Liam O'Brien's line ball was sent into the danger area for Wexford and Billy Fitzpatrick slammed it past Henry Butler from close range. Kilkenny helped themselves to three quick points, and the sides were level once more. Two points each from Matt Ruth and midfielder, Joe Hennessy finally saw the Cats win it.

The 1980s dawned, and in the next five years, Wexford would meet Kilkenny four times in the Leinster semi-final. Offaly's emergence and steely intent, and also the introduction of the open draw had put paid to the pair coasting to provincial deciders. Wexford would win two of those provincial semi-finals, and lose two. And the pair would also meet up in the 1982 National league final that Kilkenny would win by six points.

In 1980, in the semi-final, Kilkenny had a big lead on us at half-time... 10 points if I remember correctly. They scored three goals in the first-half... but we got back at them in the second-half and we might have got level.

That was the first year of what they called the 'open draw' which was a controversial move in Leinster, because... y'know, the general thing was that Wexford and Kilkenny were seeded in Leinster before then.

Oh sure, it seemed to be always written in stone that we would be in the Leinster final with them. Not to be there for the first time in over a decade was a shock to the system.

There was a small crowd in Croke Park that afternoon... less than 18,000!

We were well behind and we got back into it.

It looked to be running for us near the end, but Kilkenny regrouped. They won by five points.

I was marking Cody that day, for the first time in a championship game... it was a good old battle between us.

Losing semi-finals in Leinster was a fair shock to the systems of both teams. In the previous 30 years, Kilkenny and Wexford had met five times only at the penultimate stage in the province.

The previous meeting between the two teams, before 1980, had been in 1964, when Kilkenny repeated a win that they had also recorded in '63 at the same stage over their neighbours. When they had met in 1961, in a game Wexford won by four points, they had set a new attendance record for a Leinster semi-final of 31,636. Wexford had also accounted for Kilkenny in semi-finals in 1952 and '54, with hefty victories on both occasions, 4-7 to 0-1 and 5-11 to 0-7 respectively.

Only three times in the previous 30 years, since 1950, had either team suffered a semi-final loss to another county – Kilkenny to Laois in 1951, and Wexford to Dublin in 1959 and Offaly in 1969.

In 1980, as Doran remembers only too well, Kilkenny tore into Wexford from the very start and set the tempo for a game which saw 41 scores registered. At the end of the game, there was also disagreement about the final scoreline – the scoreboards in the stadium, several newspapermen, and even the umpires had different sets of numbers in their heads. But the referee, Gerry Kirwan from Offaly, had tallied the score in his book as Kilkenny 4-18 and Wexford 3-16.

It was an epic fightback from Wexford, who were 3-9 to 0-8 behind at half-time, and found themselves 12 points in arrears five minutes into the second-half. The Wexford comeback started with a Tony Doran point in the sixth minute of the half, and ended with a Doran goal which left just a single point between the two teams.

Kilkenny goaled at the other end, but Wexford went down fighting according to Peadar O'Brien in *The Irish Press*:

'Wexford tried gallantly to lift themselves again. Tony Doran went on another swashbuckling raid through the middle but his palmed effort was disrupted by a fierce buffeting from the Kilkenny defence and the ball was cleared.

Kinsella then showed great presence of mind to whip a pass behind the Kilkenny defence for Doran but again the ball failed to run kindly and the only reward was a '70'. Jacob, who had pointed an earlier effort from that range, went for the short one this time but a magnificent catch under the bar by Noel Skehan foiled Wexford of the goal they needed and as Wexford swept back again another effort by Courtney was saved.'

In 1981, Wexford got back into the Leinster final, and accounted for Kilkenny on their way there, a semi-final meeting on June 21 ending with a three points victory (4-12 to 1-18). But meetings between Tony Doran and Kilkenny were now coming to an end, and 'big days' especially were running out. They would not meet in the 1982 Leinster championship, Doran's third last championship in the purple and gold, but they did get together in the final of the league.

It was only the second game I played in that league campaign in '82. We beat Tipperary in the quarter-final... the first game I was back for was the semi-final against Cork.

I came back with very little training or anything done. But I played that day in Thurles, against Cork... and it was one of those days when you come back and the ball seemed to follow me around everywhere I went.

In the final against Kilkenny it was a different kettle of fish.

More or less, with work and a growing family, it did not suit me to play that winter... it was only when we got to the late spring that I started back doing a bit.

I was 36 years of age at the time as well. I think at that stage every year was nearly a bonus... definitely. You would be putting on weight at that stage... your metabolism is slowing down.

You finally realise that you might be getting old.

It had been 15 years since Wexford and Kilkenny had met in the 1967 League final, when Kilkenny were the hottest of favourites, but Wexford won with seven points to spare. In the late spring of 1982, Kilkenny were favoured once more to lift the league title.

At 36, Tony Doran indeed was the only Wexford link to that afternoon in '67, while Frank Cummins, who was a substitute for John Teehan in '67, bridged the gap for Kilkenny. In Wexford's comeback against Cork in the semi-final, Doran had plundered like old times, however, and taken two goals against John Crowley. In the league final, the meeting of Doran and Cody was one of the headliners, though it was felt that Doran would have to make the most of his chances. *'At this stage of his career,'* reported Donal Carroll in *The Irish Independent, 'the Wexford full-forward can not be expected to dance around and harry a whole defence for long periods; but all he needs, even now, is a stray chance to beat the defenders and plant the ball in the net.'* As it turned out, Cody only allowed Doran to win possession cleanly twice in the game.

Each time, Doran's shot was blocked by Noel Skehan; though with his second effort, after rounding the Kilkenny full-back, he struck the ball less fiercely than normal and sent it directly at Skehan. Either side of Cody, Dick O'Hara and John Henderson, were also alert and always on duty any time the ball descended in the Kilkenny goal area.

Kilkenny won their fifth league title by 2-14 to 1-11.

There would be two more championship meetings with Kilkenny for Tony Doran, in the Leinster semi-finals of 1983 and '84.

On June 19, 1983, Tony Doran only managed a single point over the 70 minutes against his oldest of enemies and his greatest of friends, but as Wexford captain he never stopped leading and inspiring those around him. He did so from the very start as Wexford tore into the game and were not at all flattered by a 1-10 to 1-3 lead by half-time. It took Kilkenny 25 minutes to register their first score.

The second-half was a different matter entirely, and Kilkenny were fired up. The game became heated as well and referee Jimmy Rankins of Laois saw fit to send Wexford full-back, Tony Walsh and his opponent, Christy Heffernan to the line in 46th minute.

Kilkenny would complete an heroic comeback (the deficit reached nine points at one time) to win 5-13 to 3-15, another tight four points the difference between the two counties, and Rankins found himself in some hot water at the end of game for blowing it up after only playing 60 seconds of injury time. Newspapermen had measured a full three minutes on their stop watches in the press box for the clear-up after the altercation between Walsh and Heffernan. They had also timed an injury to John Quigley at an additional 30 seconds.

One had also likened Tony Doran to a *'nimble youth'* in his duel with Brian Cody.

On an awful lot of occasions, when I look back through my career, Wexford were guilty of losing big leads against Kilkenny.

I don't know why?

A lead of seven or eight... or 10 points was really nothing... not against them!

It could disappear in a flash. Games were always high scoring anyhow. There was no such thing as defensive systems to hold onto leads or anything to that effect.

Kilkenny teams, also, had an inner belief in themselves that most other teams did not possess... they never thought a game had raced away from them.

They always saw it in their sights. That's why they would break down big leads... it wasn't just our fault or a question of Wexford teams sitting back on their big leads... it was more about Kilkenny seeing an even bigger challenge in front of them, and taking it on.

That's what makes Kilkenny so different to everyone else, and special I guess.

Tony Doran played only one game in the league campaign (a three points loss to Waterford in Enniscorthy) through the winter of 1983 and spring of 1984. It was not 'old age' or 'milking' that kept him away from the hurling field, however. He was closing in fast enough on his 40th birthday.

His body needed looking after.

I had a hernia operation just before Christmas, and I actually played the first round of the league but I had been troubled by the hernia for a few years before that.

I came on in the league against Waterford, and did not play any other league match after that. I had the operation on Christmas week in Wexford county hospital.

Nowadays, a hernia operation is a relatively minor thing, but back then you were advised to lift nothing and do nothing strenuous for about six weeks.

That was the recuperating time... and doctors' orders were doctors' orders.

I didn't start back training or doing anything until well into

April... by that stage the fellas were back in another league final, and they were doing very well... but we got a big beating from Limerick that day in Thurles.

I played a first match with the club, and it took off from there. I went back to the county team and played a few challenge matches in the lead up to the Leinster semi-final against Kilkenny, and got back in... just in time.

On June 17, 1984, Tony Doran played his last game against Kilkenny at Croke Park in the Leinster semi-final. It was a good year to still be alive and playing hurling, as the GAA celebrated its first 100 years.

Kilkenny were of a mind to mark the association's centenary year with a little bit of history of their own making, as they targeted a three in-a-row of All-Ireland titles to follow up their victories in 1982 and '83.

And Tony Doran?

He guessed it might be his last rattle at them.

And the chance to plunder one final championship goal against another iron-clad black and amber defence?

That was the dream.

I never retired, so I did not know it was the last game I'd ever play against them... but, I suppose I had a good idea it could have been my last.

I was in on Dick O'Hara, and it was level coming to the last few minutes and... I got onto the ball... and...

I can well remember it...

I caught it and got inside Dick O'Hara and I'd say I must have got a good strike on it... I was between the 14 and 21 yard lines...

I remember striking it off the left side. It was near the end of the game... couple of minutes to go, and it turned out to be the last score of the game.

It was the first time I played on Dick in the championship... I'd played on him a few times in league games. It was a tough battle... he was a big strong man, bearded, he always looked a real warrior out there...

And he was hard to beat.

We won by three points on the day, and to get that goal that made a difference... was fantastic for me personally, but the real hero of our team was Martin Fitzhenry.

I got my dream goal, but Martin... he had a dream day. He scored two goals and three points... he was making his first championship start and he was the real hero of the hour.

Tony Doran, before the Leinster semi-final against Kilkenny, had not played in a competitive game since the previous October when he had come in against Waterford. But he had squeezed in two challenge matches in as many weeks, and he had earned back his prized No.14 jersey by scoring a total of 5-4 against Waterford and Tipperary.

Every minute of Tony Doran's last game against Kilkenny, a game Wexford won by 3-10 to 1-13, were precious. Peadar O'Brien's match report in *The Irish Press* recorded it thus:

'Superlatives are totally inadequate. One can only stand at amazement and wonder how otherwise ordinary human beings can drive themselves to such feats of daring and endurance as the Wexford and Kilkenny hurlers did yesterday at Croke Park and then shrug it off as a mere game.

Yet, once again, these two counties, as they have so frequently done in the past, produced a match of extraordinary skill and sportsmanship which left the crowd of 33,061 limp with excitement and dazzled by the brilliance of a quite extraordinary spectacle.

And so Kilkenny, whose last championship defeat was also to Wexford at Croke Park back in 1981, have had their dreams of a third All-Ireland in-a-row and a centenary All-Ireland at that, shattered in a most remarkable way. They got caught in a Wexford whirlwind with which they never fully coped. They were six points to nil down after 17 minutes and fought back to level the match on three occasions, yet they never got their noses in front and were finally seen off by a Tony Doran goal, which was plucked straight out of that ageless wizard's top drawer.

In the course of the match, Kilkenny switched their players about frequently and repeatedly but to no avail. Wexford's defence buckled at times, but did not break.'

Doran's goal, two minutes from the end, finally shattered's Kilkenny great hopes. But James O'Connor at centre-back was peerless for the winners. Not far behind him in the courage department was Eamon Cleary at right corner-back. But the whole of Wexford's defence was magnificent on Tony Doran's special day – John Nolan, who made three brilliant saves, Tony Walsh, Pat Kenny, George O'Connor and Mick Jacob.

Doran also topped his performance with a couple of points, as his duel with Dick O'Hara fascinated everyone in the ground, including Peadar O'Brien in the front row of the press box in the Hogan Stand.

'He (Doran) weighed in with 1-2 so that the Kilkenny defence was never able to relax and play their normal constructive game. The battle between Dick O'Hara and Doran was an endless fascination. Doran still catches the ball over his head with all the old majesty. O'Hara could not beat him in that facet of the game but he did limit to a minimum Doran's opportunity for swinging his hurley. Had O'Hara not done so, Doran would have torn Kilkenny asunder.'

Six points up, Wexford were unlucky when Christy Heffernan was awarded a penalty. The Glenmore giant blasted the ball to the back of the net himself, and when Wexford were quickly awarded a penalty at the other end it appeared that justice would be done. But Dick O'Hara saved the shot, and his clearance was taken by Harry Ryan who tipped over a point.

After 27 minutes, Kilkenny were level. But Doran took a point and then he gained possession, saw Fitzhenry unmarked inside him, and the young man drove the ball to the net to make it 1-8 to 1-5 for Wexford, who retired at half-time with that same lead, but had John Nolan to thank after he made two exceptional saves from the Fennelly brothers. Nolan saved again after the break.

Peadar O'Brien saw the ending thus:

'Another good save by Nolan followed after the break but, after Houlihan had scored a splendid point from the sideline and Heffernan had been satisfied with a point from a penalty, Fitzhenry struck again.

This time the Kilkenny defence was put into a fine old dither by Doran and when the ball was only partially cleared, Fitzhenry grabbed it and palmed it into the net deceiving Skehan in the process.

Kilkenny moved Kieran Brennan to centre forward at this stage and a revival got underway. Fitzpatrick converted two frees and a Ryan shot for goal was deflected over the bar by Nolan – his best save of the day. Fitzpatrick had another free and Kieran Brennan raced through a suddenly slack Wexford defence for a point.

There was danger now of too many excited 'mentors' getting into the action in the Wexford goal after a foul on Nolan and with 10 minutes left for play, Ray Heffernan, who had replaced Fitzpatrick, brought Kilkenny level.

Sean Kinsella and Kieran Brennan swapped points as the excitement reached a new peak. First Johnny Murphy missed a shot near goal and then Billy Byrne missed as well. At the other end, the tireless Joe Hennessy raced through but missed for Kilkenny. Then Byrne placed Doran, who grabbed the ball and struck the goal with all his old deadly aplomb.

Two minutes to go. Kilkenny are awarded a penalty and Heffernan goes for goal but somehow it is swept away by a forest of Wexford hurleys. Then comes a '70' and again the ball is under the Wexford bar but this time Cleary bats it out and clears it away as the final whistle releases the throngs from the terraces at the end of an unforgettable match.'

It was always Kilkenny.

It began with Kilkenny for Tony Doran, and so it ended with a goal and a famous victory over Kilkenny.

There would be no more for Wexford in 1984, however, a one point Leinster final defeat awaiting the team the following month – and awaiting Tony Doran as he played his last game for Wexford on the old sod in Croke Park.

He would end his career with a head full of memories of more Kilkenny full-backs than full-backs from any other county.

Starting off, it was Pa Dillon... then Nicky Orr... they were probably the two more regular fellas I met up with on the field. But there was Brian Cody near the end... Fan Larkin of course... Fan was normally a corner-back but I would have played on him as well when he was in at 'full'.

In the earlier days there was also Jim Lynch... and then Dick O'Hara near the end... Paddy Prendergast might have been in on me once or twice as well.

Another fella from St Martin's too ... Jim Moran!

There were a good few of them... I might be forgetting one or two of them as well, I'm sure... but there was a good supply of full-backs in the black and amber, put it that way!

Starting off as a young lad and all, it wasn't easy coming up against Pa Dillon... Pa had a name for being one of the toughest men at the time. But y'know, hitting up against him in those first five or six years for Wexford... that was probably where I learned most about the whole game.

Nicky Orr came after him and was a different type of a player completely... he wasn't as big... didn't quite have the same reputation or presence, I suppose, as Pa did.

Nevertheless, Nicky Orr was effective. He might not have been a stylish hurler but he was good in getting the ball out of the danger area.

Dillon was, I suppose, my apprenticeship... he was regarded as a bit of tough man, but the nicest man you could hit up against off the field.

Cody, sure... he was more of a hurling type and then at that stage the game was changing as well... it was a different proposition... and Cody was playing a different game to the men before him. He would be trying to get out in front of me to win the ball... whereas before him full-backs would be more content to mind their square and stay between me and the goals.

The one match that stands out? Against them... against the Cats?

There's not one... a few matches maybe stand out more than anything... because, don't forget, we played them so often... in championship every year, in Walsh Cups which were regarded as a big thing at that time... we'd go to Kilkenny to play them, they'd come to Wexford... and they were all important matches. There might be seven or eight thousand at some of those matches... the likes of Oireachtas matches.

We had them in the league nearly every year as well, so I was playing Kilkenny at least three times a year. I might have played against them 70, 80 times, I suppose before it was all over.

I played against them so often, that I was more familiar with them than any other team. Then, of course we were playing with the Kilkenny fellas in Leinster Railway Cup teams.

We knew one another inside out... there were no secrets, and I suppose that's why games between us were so tight nearly all the time.

Any day that Wexford ever beat Kilkenny, that was a day you'd remember.

I would reckon the '76 Leinster final... when we beat them for the first time in six years was an amazing day, not withstanding the fact that we beat them by 17 points... the fact that we actually beat them at all.

Because I'd say a couple of our biggest disappointments in that period were against Kilkenny also. I know drawing with Kilkenny in the '72 Leinster final was a big disappointment to me... losing by a point in the '74 final was another major blow.

Did it all balance out a bit in the end? I don't know if it did.

They are the biggest power in the game... in the history of hurling, and they were our neighbours... there was no escaping them.

We had a reasonable run at it... a reasonable number of good days.

Chapter 11

The 1981 Leinster final was very short, and not very sweet, for Tony Doran. Wexford had held firm against Kilkenny in the semi-final and held out for a three points win and, as always with the Cats out of the way; behind them, forgotten about for another few months at least, the road ahead looked… well, limitless.

It was the shortest Leinster final of Tony Doran's long life in purple and gold, and most of it is remembered approximately three miles from Croke Park, as Doran lay on a bed in Jervis Street Hospital in the centre of the city.

I wasn't there too long… in Croker!

I got knocked out early on, after about 10 minutes… I guess.

I got hit across the side of the head with a stick… and I didn't even get a free!

I have no idea what happened and I'm not saying anyone did anything wrong. I have no idea, even still, what happened that afternoon.

But I was knocked out stone cold.

Only time I ever had to go off in a match. I was stretchered off... though I can vaguely remember going off on that stretcher. I was brought out by the side of the Nally Stand, somewhere around there... and brought to hospital in an ambulance.

It was either Jervis Street or the Mater... I can't be sure which of them it was? But I think it was Jervis Street, which is closed a long time now.

And I remember being half-in and half-out of it when I got to the hospital. They brought me in... me still in my gear and everything was still really foggy in my head.

I was obviously still coming and going... not fully conscious.

I think I was lying on a bench or a bed... or whatever the hell I was lying on... but I remember coming to... I can't recall still which hospital? But anyhow I came to and... I was looking for a radio to find out how the match was going?

A nurse got one for me... one that was very bad reception... I could barely make out what was happening. It was coming to the closing stages of the match.

The second-half was well in and we were three or four points behind, and one of the first things I heard was that we got a goal (scored by my brother, Colm from outfield)... and that brought it back to a single point.

There were a couple of minutes to go... I was fairly well back to my senses at this stage, I think... and trying to keep up with what was going on.

I could hear Micheal O'Mhuircheartaigh shouting. Padge Courtney had the ball in the middle of the field... and Micheal was shouting...

'THE SIDES ARE...'...

And he was about to shout... 'LEVEL!'

And then I heard ...

'NO... NO... NO...

'IT'S GONE WIDE!'

Time was nearly up and from the puck out Offaly went down

the field and got another point.

I was on my own in the hospital.

There was no one with me... Mary was not at the match that day. I got out after a few hours... didn't have to stay the night.

They stitched me up.

The other lads who had travelled with me to the match, the lads from the Alley... they came into the hospital afterwards.

I went home with them.

Their Leinster final victory over Wexford was another historic step for Offaly, in a truly historic year. In September of 1981 they would, finally, and deservedly, be crowned All-Ireland champions. Their victory over Wexford was recorded in *The Irish Independent* by Donal Carroll thus:

'Offaly's hurlers silenced their last remaining critics with a sometimes dynamic display of power-packed hurling at cool, dry but overcast Croke Park yesterday before an attendance of 29,053. They staved off the gutsy challenge of Wexford and in retaining the Leinster title they won initially a year ago qualified for the All-Ireland final for the first Sunday in September, for the first time in their history.

One uses the qualifying word 'sometimes' because Offaly hit valley periods during which they looked very ordinary indeed and these were the spells during which handicapped Wexford threatened to take control. Wexford suffered their setback only 16 minutes into the game when Tony Doran was removed to hospital with a badly gashed forehead.

Tony Doran went down in a bout of fierce pulling, but while the referee Noel O'Donoghue spoke to an Offaly defender, he stopped short of administering a booking. Doran had been having a pretty lean time of it up till then, as Offaly moved in smartly under every dropping ball, to ensure the Wexford dangerman was hemmed in on all sides.

With Tony Doran's departure Offaly changed their tactics, and given that extra bit of 'room' Wexford celebrated to be but a point adrift at the halfway stage. ...'

The previous year, 1980, Kilkenny had been waiting to lift the Leinster title for the 50th time, when they were knocked off their feet by one of their own.

Diarmuid Healy, a Kilkennyman, and a newspaperman in the county, had thrown in his lot with Offaly before the '80 campaign. That summer commenced for the Faithful county with a first win over Dublin since 1909, and even then it was a struggle to get the attendance at Croke Park on the afternoon of the Leinster final against Kilkenny to top the 10,000 mark.

'We probably assumed we could beat them,' Pat Henderson, who had just retired, and was positioned as a joint manager with Eddie Keher, would later confide. 'Our focus was always on Wexford and we had some royal battles with them during the 70s. But, on the day we had no answer to Offaly, even though it was close on the scoreboard.' Both Henderson and Keher were not forgiven for that defeat, and as a partnership their time was up.

'Offaly had a new flair and style,' Henderson would admit to *The Sunday Independent*, '... any tricks we had, they could do better. In Kilkenny, people looked on us losing rather than Offaly winning. We had nothing to offer; usually, Kilkenny would pull something out of the bag.'

'We knew some of their older players like Padraig Horan and Johnny Flaherty but there were all these young players, relatively unknown to us, flying all over the place.'

Healy, who would later become Chief Executive of Radio Kilkenny, knew that Kilkenny folk would be understanding. 'Kilkenny people have hurling at heart,' he told the *Independent*. 'Certainly they wouldn't want to see Kilkenny being beaten and would be very parochial in supporting their team, yet at the same time when they saw a new county coming through it was acceptable. If it was Tipp or Wexford (beating Kilkenny) that would be a different story.'

Henderson had played in 10 All-Ireland finals, and won five, in his career that commenced in 1964, and he would return to prove his mettle by leading the black and amber to league and championship doubles in 1982 and '83 – the first of which would include a controversial victory over Offaly.

'They should have beaten us in 1969 (Leinster final) but Pat Delaney from my own club got three goals,' Henderson continued in his chat with *The Sunday Independent*. 'They had a fine side but didn't have the organisation right. A bit inclined to be over-zealous, let's put it like that, which meant they gave away too many frees. But after 1980 we were on our guard in every match.

'Wexford were our outstanding rivals of the time. We feared Wexford more than Munster, even though Limerick beat us (in the 1973 All-Ireland final).

We felt that if we could beat Wexford we had a good chance of winning the All-Ireland.'

The rivalry between Kilkenny and Offaly was in its infancy, but it was a healthy one. In the 70s, while Henderson was still playing for Kilkenny, he recalled that the Offaly coach, Andy Gallagher, and their star full-forward Padraig Horan and a few others, would be amongst the attendance at Kilkenny training sessions looking in and learning.

It was Kilkenny that Offaly decided to try to mirror!

'Offaly always had great admiration for Kilkenny hurling,' Healy concluded. Henderson was in agreement. 'I think it's a healthy rivalry,' he commented, 'the teams would respect each other without fearing each other. Offaly feel that if they can play well that they can beat Kilkenny, and Kilkenny would feel the same way. They are similar in terms of style and approach.'

Offaly, at the very beginning of the 1980s, were a team to be respected, and reckoned with. Wexford would lose to them once again, in 1982, by a point (2-16 to 3-12).

Offaly had being going hard in the few years before that. In '79 we had only beaten them by a point in the Leinster semi-final... they beat Kilkenny and won their first Leinster title in '80... and they beat us and won their first All-Ireland in '81. So that Offaly team at the time were at the peak of their powers.

They were a good strong team.

It was a line-ball from Paddy Kirwan, if I remember in '82... a line-ball from under the Cusack Stand and he put it over the bar for the winner.

We had led, probably, with 10 minutes to go and were three points up, and it looked like we were going to do it. But Offaly came back, got a few points to level it... they then got their winner. We had a few chances after that, couple of long range frees... 50, 60 yards out to level it and missed both of them.

There was nothing in it really on the day. But they had worked very, very hard to get to where they were.

Offaly were another new force, and it was no longer just the same old two in Leinster hurling. That, and the open draw, changed everything... everything was shaken up completely.

Wexford would beat Kilkenny by three points in the Leinster semi-final in 1984, and find themselves with Offaly in the provincial decider.

It was Tony Doran's last game in the championship.

His last game in Croker in the purple and gold!

It was another match, quite like matches against Kilkenny down through the years, that was watertight. One point would split the teams after 70 minutes.

It was also another afternoon that ended in some controversy as a Kilkennyman, asked to referee a Leinster final between two of his own county's hottest rivals, found himself the centre of discussion. In the press box, the consensus was that Paschal Long sounded his final whistle prematurely.

Second-half delays, after injuries to Wexford's Eamon Cleary and Offaly's Aidan Fogarty had amounted to a full three minutes, according to men in the press box. The referee, however, only allowed one minute and five seconds of 'injury time' and although Offaly looked the better team for two-thirds of the contest, it was felt that Wexford had been denied the opportunity of staging a grandstand conclusion to the match.

Tony Doran was not the type of man to become sentimental, or one to look for sympathy at the end of any 70 minutes. The game ended with Offaly on 1-15, and Wexford on 2-11, and Doran was the sort of man who believed that the full 70 minutes were there to ensure that the best team won most matches.

Besides, Offaly had led from start to finish in the match – and they had eight points on the board before Padge Courtney opened the Wexford account 10 minutes before the interval. But that score, and the decision to move George O'Connor from right half-back to midfield, and Martin Quigley from the left wing to centre-forward, afforded Wexford a foothold in Tony Doran's last Leinster final.

Wexford scored four points in the next three minutes. Wexford trailed by three, 0-6 to 0-9, at half-time. The second-half skipped by, as life seems to skip by the older you get, and when the match came to a close Tony Doran was the last to complain.

Maybe he knew, in his heart, that there would be another glorious afternoon back in Croke Park.

Just one more?

The match ended prematurely in '84... or so they say anyhow.

You have no idea how much time was left when you're out there... it's only afterwards that you learn that it ended a bit faster than people thought it should have ended.

Whether it would have made any difference or not, we'll never know. I was on Eugene Coughlan that day... big athletic man... I scored one point which was disappointing.

Offaly got off to a big start and were eight points to no score up before we got out of the traps.

They also believed that they had a future... that they had matches to win... and championships, and All-Ireland titles.

They were hungry... fierce hungry, and you could see it, sense it I suppose.

It was their turn... their opportunity, and they took it. Like everyone else, I was happy to see a new team turn the corner.

It's good for the game... hurling needs fresh blood. There are too few teams that are really competitive.

Wexford, I'm happy to say... we gave it everything we had all the years I was lucky enough to wear the jersey. We were hungry too, and I think we deserved to win more than we did.

But... I'd never complain. We got the chance to stand our ground and fight it out... with the very best of them.

Chapter 12

I've never considered myself retired.

There was never any announcement... none made by me anyhow... but you know yourself.

In 1985 I was up in the stand when Wexford were beaten by Laois in the Leinster semi-final.

We lost by two points.

And in the Leinster final that summer you had Offaly and Laois, imagine that? Just a few years before that... and right through the 70s, Kilkenny and ourselves had met up in every single Leinster final... for 10 years in-a-row.

It was like we owned the whole thing. But in the second-half of the 80s, sure Wexford only got to the Leinster final once... in '88... when we lost to Offaly again.

Time moves on fast.

Of course, in 1986 I was still playing with the club and Buffers Alley went the whole way to the All-Ireland club final, and had been beaten in it. Our own John Doyle from the Alley was Wexford manager that year and he was getting onto me... about giving it a shot again.

I thought about it... but I was only sort of half-hearted about it to be honest.

I went to a couple of training sessions with the county, and they went alright.

After that, Wexford were playing a challenge match against Waterford one night down in the south of the county... and I told John I'd go down to that and I'd make my mind up after that.

The game was in Bannow... and I went down, but as it was, Wexford only had a second team out and I played. But, after that, I said... 'John... No way!'

I had started the game, but I got onto John the next day and told him that I did not believe I could make it... told him I was pulling out of it. Wexford were due to play Kilkenny in a Leinster semi-final a few weeks after, but I felt that I wasn't at the pace of it.

And I wasn't.

There were a good few new players coming into the team and I was not familiar with them... and I told John that it was their turn.

I stayed playing with the club... and John accepted my decision. The following Sunday after I had spoken to him, the Alley were playing a tournament match against someone... can't remember who... and I scored five goals and two points.

It was one of them days... I seemed to be flying. But I was 40 years of age.

However, I had made my mind up. I did not give it a another thought. I never did announce anything publicly.

Why? I don't know... but probably because nobody ever asked me!

Only time I was ever asked about retiring was a little time before that after the club All-Ireland final in Croker, and this journalist came into the room and sat down beside me and I knew him fairly well. He was a good fella... someone I liked.

He asked me if I was retiring?

But we'd just been beaten in an All-Ireland club final and I was not in the mood for that conversation.

I told him what to do with himself.

'Is that it now?'

That's what the poor man has asked me, innocently enough.

He got it with both barrels... poor fella. I think he got a bit of a fright.

He went off with his tail between his legs, but there were a lot of other journalists close by and they overheard our conversation.

I can only imagine they got a bit of a land as well... with my angry reply to the question.

Nobody ever asked me again.

Epilogue

In the replay to the 1988 Wexford senior hurling final Buffers Alley decided it was time to put a stop to playing second fiddle to Rathnure. They won by double scores, 2-10 to 1-5, and those present in Wexford Park agreed that the scoreline did not do justice to the difference between the teams. Buffers Alley hurled their greatest, and proudest, of enemies off the park.

They did so in conditions which, locals still claim, were the toughest ever presented on the afternoon of a county final. Half the pitch was under water. The remainder of the field was a muddied test that Tony Doran and his comrades decided to totally ignore.

They had already beaten us in one, two, three, four, five... six county finals, between 1967 and '86... in so many finals... it was unreal... and in the first game in 1988 Rathnure were nine points up at half-time. They had the breeze, but it looked only a 'three or four points breeze' and we looked dead and buried.

We got a draw out of it... back level in less than 15 minutes and it was tit for tat after that... and sure enough it ended level. The bogey was still there... we had not beaten Rathnure in a county senior final and we had to go back the following week for the replay.

And, who'd believe it... we beat them well... and it looked like we had achieved everything... we had beaten Rathnure in a county final! I felt at that stage... maybe... I was ready to leave it.

I was marking Martin Quigley the first day... but then I was moved to corner-forward and Mick Butler went in full-forward on Martin. I moved to the corner and got a goal that started to bring us back into the game... and for the replay Rathnure decided to move Martin onto me in the corner... where I started.

And it worked to our advantage because we had Martin away from their goal. I scored a goal off him early on.

It was absolutely a pouring wet day, but we didn't worry about that. The celebrations after that final were incredible... to have beaten them in the final... it was unbelievable.

A handful of us had played against Rathnure when they had beaten us in the first final in '67... myself, Henry Butler, Mick Butler, Martin Casey.... and my brother, Colm, who always had back trouble, was a sub in that final... a handful of us were there the whole way.

The sight of them had been enough all down through those years. They were really strong. It wasn't a case of us thinking we couldn't beat them... we weren't able to beat them.

They were always strong... all the time, and they had three or four county men the whole time who won so many games for them. They had won several Leinster titles... but no All-Ireland. They were beaten in four or five finals... and narrowly on occasions.

They were unlucky they didn't win one.

It had rained non-stop for two days prior to the replayed final. Some players swore that in some parts of the field they found themselves ankle-deep. The Alley had the wind at their backs in the first-half.

They took full advantage of it, shooting five points in the opening eight minutes of the game. Tony Doran and Mick Butler were leading the charge. It was 0-6 to 0-1. In the Rathnure goal Ted Morrissey made three remarkable saves before Seamus O'Leary, coming in from the right, collected the ball smoothly, and drilled home a shot from 25 yards out. Rathnure then lost Jimmy Holohan to a hand injury (though Buffers Alley lost centre-back Mattie Foley with a head injury), but before they could even think about plotting a massive comeback, Tony Doran did what Tony Doran simply did so often on the biggest stage.

Doran got onto the end of a passage of play between Butler and Martin Casey, and took his goal with typically modest aplomb. The half-time whistle was due, but Buffers Alley were 2-8 to 0-2 in front

The game was effectively over.

The Alley only managed two points in the second-half, but it was more than enough on this historic day that had kept hurling folk in Monamolin and Kilmuckridge waiting for so long.

Tony Doran and Buffers Alley had one more shot at an All-Ireland title. But, of course, a number of years before 1989 they had become the first and only Wexford team to win the All-Ireland club title – Buffers Alley had once upon a time planted the flag of their parish on the national stage for everyone to see and admire.

That was 16 years earlier, back in 1973 when, the day before the All-Ireland final itself, the very first Kilmacud Crokes All-Ireland 'Sevens' competition was staged in south county Dublin.

It was a famous day in Buffers Alley history.

It was also an infamous day in the legendary career of Tony Doran, as it was the only time in his long and brilliant career that he stood over a free.

When he is asked some decades later why he never took a free for Buffers Alley or Wexford, Doran is disarmingly self-mocking. He claims he was never up to the task, and that there were always others, in the green and gold of the Alley, and others again in the Purple and gold of Wexford, who had a sharper eye.

It is genuinely hard to believe him.

I was never up to it... I'd say that was about the size of it.

From my earliest days, with the club and everything else, I was never regarded as a free-taker. I never got into the art of free-taking to be quite honest. I don't know if I would have been any good at it... I might have been bad at it.

I remember only taking a free with the club once, and that was in the All-Ireland 'Sevens' final, and I got a point from the free... the only free I ever took in my life.

It was about 60 yards out... sort of to one side. I remember I put the ball down and I wouldn't let anyone else near it.

We were playing St Finbarr's from Cork in the final. It was a see-saw game against the 'Barrs... and they had all of their star players... Ger McCarthy, Tony Maher... fellas like that... though we had a good auld team as well.

It was a couple of minutes near the end, and I won the ball and got fouled about 60 yards out near the sideline. Mick Butler was taking frees for us but he was gone off at the time.

He wasn't on the field.

I just dropped the ball onto the ground and stood over it. I recall Joe... my brother, Joe... running over to me, and wanting to take the free.

But I ran him!

It would never have occurred to anyone that I would take it, but... when I was standing over it, I decided that nobody else was going to take it. I told him to go away... but used stronger language than that.

I remember the strike.

It went straight over the black spot.

Maybe there are times when you feel something inside you, and I just knew at that moment... I was convinced that I was going to put the ball over the bar.

Mick Butler always took the frees for the club. When I started with the Alley first, Bill Murphy took the frees... and he was a very, very good free-taker. When he retired, Mick took over... because

Mick had been taking them all along, in underage and all.

And if Mick was injured?

Mick was very seldom injured... if I remember.

At the start with Wexford, Paul Lynch would have been the free-taker... in-chief... moving on from that, Ned Buggy would have been taking them a lot of the time. If Ned was playing in the back line, Mick Butler would have taken over, and Tom Byrne would have taken them too.

Jack Berry was a bit like myself. Neither of us wanted to take them all that much. And down through all those years, I never scored from a free for Wexford... not a single point.

The All-Ireland 'Sevens' was not even in its infancy.

It was the very birth of a competition that would very quickly capture the imagination of club teams all over the country, who wished on the eve of the All-Ireland final to have their say.

Limerick would defeat Kilkenny, 1-21 to 1-14 in Croke Park the next day, Richie Bennis striking 10 points, Mossie Dowling blasting their goal, but 24 hours earlier the Dorans were busy harvesting barley. Tony and Colm had promised that they would turn up in Kilmacud for the tournament, but it turned out Saturday morning was more tempting as a working day and not a hurling day.

The sun was shining.

And the two lads got to work. They had no choice really as Bill, who would normally be the man in charge of the harvesting, had been injured in a club match the previous week and was hobbling about the place in plaster. With Bill Doran out of commission, and the sun shining, hurling had to be placed on the back burner. There had been a short enough discussion over breakfast.

Work?

Or go to Dublin, and hurl?

In 1973, nobody had a mobile phone handy. Nobody in the world of big business had even imagined such an item attached to someone's hip or dropped into a breast-pocket of a work shirt.

Tony and Colm were hard at work before they knew it, and they had no idea whatsoever when they were supposed to be reporting to Kilmacud for the All-Ireland 'Sevens'.

It was fairly late... and we said, 'Feck it... we'll go'.

When we were leaving home the first game should have been on or thereabouts. The other lads were gone a long time, and they did not have the numbers to take part. There were only six of them who had headed up to Dublin... and they needed the two of us, and John Stamp who also arrived to go up with us.

That made nine of us.

We headed up anyhow, and I'll tell you now we hit the road in spots on the way up to Kilmacud. Whatever we were driving it wasn't top of the range either. We belted up, the three of us, accompanied by our neighbour, Bernard Kavanagh who was one of our few supporters on the day... and we landed in Kilmacud, and they were just getting ready to take the field for the first match and Ger Dempsey, our chief mentor... Ger must have been in his 50s... he was ready to make up the seventh man when we landed.

We were playing Glen Rovers, no less... the cream of Cork... players like Denis Coughlan, Gerry O'Sullivan. The match was delayed for a few seconds while we jumped into the gear.

Buffers Alley won by a single point.

Two more wins followed in the early afternoon. Buffers Alley found themselves in the All-Ireland semi-final... a 'Sevens' final, but an All-Ireland semi-final nevertheless. They beat Mooncoin.

St Finnbarr's won their way through from the other side of the draw to the final also. Buffers Alley V's the 'Barrs!

And because Cork were not playing in the All-Ireland final in Croke Park the next day the 'Barrs had brought all of their first-choice men from Cork to Dublin with them. Buffers Alley defeated the best of Cork.

Tony Doran scored a point from an outrageous free. But the fact that he actually took a free was as big a talking point as the sliotar actually dropping over the black spot.

The Alley were All-Ireland champs.

The three Doran brothers, three Butlers, Mick Kinsella, John Stamp and Larry Harney had the distinction of being the first ever Kilmacud Crokes All-Ireland hurling champs.

Sixteen years before they officially became All-Ireland champs!

I suppose we were knackered alright, but we headed for home after the game... and we were back for the All-Ireland final the following day to see Limerick and Kilkenny in the final.
We didn't really think a lot of it!

The path to All-Ireland glory on St Patrick's Day in 1989 appeared a little uneven when Buffers Alley staggered past Carlow Town in the first round of the Leinster championship. The underdogs, in their own patch, had the temerity to put four goals past Henry Butler and Co. Same afternoon, Tony Doran was held scoreless. Two goals from Fintan O'Leary and one from Tom Dempsey had the Alley 3-6 to 1-2 in front at half-time, but as the clock was winding down in the second-half there was only three points between the teams. Then Brendan Hayden pegged another point back for Carlow, but the steadying hand of Tony Doran in the last minute set up Mick Butler for the goal that clinched victory. But 5-8 to 4-6 did not spell out very serious intentions from the Wexford champs to go all the way.

Coming on as a second-half substitute, it would also be Colm Doran's last appearance in a Buffers Alley jersey.

We got a scare a week after the county final, got that scare against Carlow Town, and we just managed to pull it out in the last few minutes. We played Seir Kiernan of Offaly in the Leinster semi-final and again it was tough and tight. We won by five points in the end, but again it was a game that could have gone any way... they had Dooleys and Coughlans, and a right good bunch so they were very strong. In the Leinster final we were hitting up against

Shamrocks... the Fennellys, so... we knew what was ahead of us.

The win over Seir Kiernan in Athy was only hammered home five minutes from the end when Sean Whelan's sideline puck went straight to the net. It was a fortuitous score that helped the Alley over the finish line on a bitterly cold day. A Tom Dempsey free and a Martin Casey point left it 1-12 to 1-7. Tony Doran grabbed two points. No goals on Eugene Coughlan who wore the Seir Kiernan No.3 shirt.

We had a big half-time lead against Shamrocks, after playing with the wind... and they clawed back at us in the second-half but we closed it out and won by three points in the end.

Despite defeating Shamrocks 1-12 to 1-9, and seeing the All-Ireland title within their sights (Roscommon's Four Roads and O'Donovan Rossa from Antrim would upset the odds and remain standing in the Alley's way) there was still a long way to go before claiming the title of All-Ireland champions. The Alley had won their fair share of county titles, and managed to come out in Leinster on only two occasions, so the likes of Tony Doran and every man in their dressing-room knew that there was nothing easy once they ever crossed the Wexford border and met worthy champs from any other county. In getting by Shamrocks, once again on the heavy sod in Dr Cullen Park in Carlow, they had had to dig deep, and deeper still.

The Alley dominated the first-half, but the Kilkenny men came back hard and strong on the resumption and the magnificent free-taking of their midfielder, Ger Fennelly put the fear of God into the winners. But Buffers Alley had claimed their second provincial crown because of two outrageously memorable scores that knocked the wind out of their opponents on each occasion.

The first, in the 10th minute of the game, came when Tony Doran rose highest to fetch a Tom Dempsey lob and turned on a sixpence as he landed, and fired the ball past a stunned and helpless Kevin Fennelly in the Shamrocks' goal. The second score arrived, smartly enough, right on full time when the Alley were clinging onto a two points advantage. Again, it was one of the 'oldies' on the team, Mick Butler who had the head and craft to slice a point from 45 yards out as he stood close to the sideline. The Leinster title was secure, but there was not much time to celebrate and the team's trainer, Fr Jim Butler wanted everyone back at it on St Stephen's Day for an All-Ireland semi-final that was almost two months off.

In the club's commemorative booklet, that would be published 25 years later to mark the one and only time a Wexford team had lifted the All-Ireland club championship, Fr Butler remembered the smiles and the sense of exhilaration when news came through to their dressing-room in Wexford Park - after they had seen off Four Roads impressively by 2-19 to 0-9 – that the Belfast lads, O'Donovan Rossa, had caused a major upset in the other All-Ireland semi-final. 'I can still see the smiles in the dressing-room… when word filtered through that the Munster champions, Patrickswell of Limerick, had been beaten in Kilmallock by O'Donovan Rossa of Antrim in the other semi-final. The scene was now set for an occasion that many believed they would never again see – Buffers Alley back in Croke Park on St Patrick's Day for the All-Ireland club hurling final.'

The Antrim champs got off to a flyer. If the Alley had any designs on claiming a handy All-Ireland, they were dispelled in those opening minutes of the All-Ireland final.

The day went fairly well for me… went pretty well… no goals, a few points had to do. We did not start off well, and we were very slow when you would have thought we'd be the quicker team out of the blocks… Croke Park… and all of that. We went four or five points down early on and had to claw that back.

The Alley had started the game with the 'quick switch' that had become quite normal since the county final victory. Tony Doran wandered into the corner, and Mick Butler made the opposite trek to the edge of the square. But as Wexford supporters settled into their seats, O'Donovan Rossa seized the afternoon early and after 10 minutes they were 0-6 to 0-1 in front. The situation might have been far worse only for Henry Butler's wits in the goalmouth. He had a half dozen excellent blocks, one of them a reflex save from point blank range in the fifth minute. In front of him, there was some chaos. The Antrim boys were faster than anyone had thought and they were pouring through the middle of the Alley defence. Their Allstar and team leader, Ciaran Barr had three points to his name. On the sideline, however, the Alley's mentors did not panic. Matty Foley and Paul Gahan swapped positions. Soon after, Tom Dempsey and Eamonn Sinnott would do the same. Fr Butler remembered in his writings a quarter of a century later how the team rebuilt itself on the field. 'Gahan plugged the gaps down the middle and snuffed out Barr, whereas Dempsey won much more midfield ball and ensured a greater supply to the forwards. The all-important score came in the 14th minute when Mick Butler flicked on an Eamonn Sinnott centre and Seamus O'Leary burst his way through to plant the ball to the net.'

It was 1-5 to 0-7 at half-time – after failing to get a goal after doing all the hard work, Tony Doran won a high ball and turned and pointed – but more work remained to be done, and it was vitally important that the Alley did not let their speedy opponents run rings around them a second time once they got back out on the field for the start of the second-half. It wasn't going to happen. Dempsey settled everyone with two pointed frees. In between, Seamus O'Leary broke through the Rossa defence again and the sliotar fell to Paddy Donohoe who whacked home the game's winning score. O'Donovan Rossa were a beaten team.

Buffers Alley 2-12, O'Donovan Rossa 0-12.

The Alley team on that proudest of days was: Henry Butler; Barry Murphy, Pat Kenny, John O'Leary; Paul Gahan, Mattie Foley, Colin Whelan; Eamonn Sinnott, Sean Whelan; Tom Dempsey, Martin Casey, Paddy Donohoe; Mick Butler, Tony Doran, Seamus O'Leary. Subs: Ben Martin, John Donohoe, John Gahan, Fintan O'Leary, Marney Burke, Matt Furlong, Harry Lee, Ger Sweeney, Colm Doran.

The difference on the final scoreline should have been more but the Alley appeared to be holding their breath for the final 15 minutes of the game. However, soon enough the historic moment arrived, and Buffers Alley captain, Pat Kenny was holding the Tommy Moore Cup high over his head on the steps of the Hogan Stand.

'The sight of a Wexford man receiving the cup of victory after achieving

All-Ireland senior hurling success was something we hadn't seen since 1968,' wrote Fr Butler. 'And while Tony Doran had been part of that great occasion, and Mick Butler and Martin Casey also had special links with that day, half of the Buffers Alley players were too young to even remember it. In fact, a whole generation of young Wexford people had grown up without knowing a moment like this. Defeat had been Wexford's lot so often on the big days that we began to believe that it was all we deserved and that we were destined to forever be second best.'

Colm Doran had missed out on being part of the magnificent day as a player. He had been in hospital for back surgery, but he defied his doctor's orders to get himself to Croke Park for the proudest day in the club's history. 'And speaking of the Dorans,' remembered Fr Butler, 'this victory had one other special significance. For the club's most famous son it was the crowing glory in an illustrious career, and it saw Tony Doran, who had been such an inspiration to Buffers Alley teams for over a quarter of a century, add that one elusive medal to his already tremendously impressive collection.'

The new All-Ireland champs were feted to a civic reception by Gorey Town Commissioners the following evening. It is estimated that over 1,000 people were on the Main Street of the town as the team, led by their captain, paraded behind the St Michael's Pipe Band. The celebrations continued for several weeks. And then another Wexford senior championship commenced.

One which the Alley would successfully defend, beating down the challenge of a tenacious Oulart The Ballagh after a replay, 3-16 to 2-13.

They would win again in 1991 with six points to spare over Faythe Harriers, and in '92 when another six points broke the hearts of Oulart The Ballagh one more time. Though in the next 25 years Buffers Alley would not win the Wexford senior hurling title again. Rathnure would claim five more and Oulart The Ballagh would forever cross the threshold and leave their role as gallant losers far behind them by proving themselves the best in Wexford 13 times.

And Tony Doran has watched it all.

He was one month away from his 43rd birthday when Buffers Alley won the All-Ireland title in 1989.

The years were passing faster than ever before. In fact, at the start of the

1988 championship he was more than half-thinking of giving it all up.

I suppose I was being carried along and didn't talk or think about retiring... but I did think about what I was doing at the beginning of 1988. Fr Jim Butler was back training us... he had been away for a few years.

But he was back training us again, and I recall early in the year... February maybe... we were playing a challenge match at home in our home pitch... against Gorey, just to start off the whole year.

No great training or anything before that... and when I left home I said to myself I'd throw my gear in the car... and see how they are for numbers?

And I was walking towards the dressing-room... going through the car park with my hands down by my sides, when Fr Jim asked me where was my gear?

'Ah... there's enough young lads here!' I replied to him, '... time to give them a chance.'

'Go back and get the bag!' Fr Jim ordered.

'We'll have none of that talk!' he added for good measure.

That was the start of the year in '88... and we did everything that we did after that, playing 14 games in all in the championship... and ending up with the All-Ireland.

In '89 we won the championship again and we beat Oulart in the county final which was a bit extra to beat our neighbours... in a replay and after extra time. Went on to Leinster and came a cropper against Cuala in a replay... games were starting to catch up at this stage.

In '90 I played senior... but in '91 I played junior. I was playing with Wexford over 40s as well at the time... playing a good bit of hurling as it happened and, in the county senior final, I came on as a sub halfway through the second-half against the Harriers.

That was my last county senior final... played in the club championship, in the latter stages... against Birr in Leinster in a semi-final when we were a couple of lads short and that was the last day I played with the Alley seniors.

My final game?

The following year... in '92... I played with the juniors and we went to county final again... lost by a point to Fethard in Wexford Park... but the match was not played till January of '93.

That was my final game... what was I?

Must have been 46... going on 47.

I enjoyed every single game... I did, right to the end. If they had been a chore at that stage I wouldn't have been there... yah, even junior... I was enjoying it and... sure for lads out there playing, it was same as senior to them... old lads... fellas who were junior all of their lives, and young fellas on the way up.

Sure, for those lads playing hurling out there... those matches are every bit as important to them as any senior match. There was great enjoyment to be got out of it still at that stage

Always nice to get a score... and when I think back on it now, the fact is that it is much easier to keep going as a forward rather than a back.

As a forward all you have to do is try to get a few scores... as opposed to playing in the backs and trying to stop them.

Easier for a forward to keep an edge.

I reckon anyway.

Tony Doran would have been happy to continue playing... forever. But his wife, Mary was at home with five children. Therese was 13 years-old in 1993. Noelle was 12, and Tony junior was almost 10. Pat was eight years old and, the youngest in the family, Marie, had been born two weeks before Tony Doran had played in his last Wexford hurling final.

As I say to a lot of people, I have not really retired yet.

There was no announcement.

I stopped... that's all that happened. It was time to cop on, I suppose. I had no big reason to stop playing..... no one big thing...

like injury or anything like that... I just stopped playing.

At that stage the youngsters were busy going around to matches and playing matches... and myself and Mary... one of us was a full time taxi driver.

Tony Doran does not mind saying that he missed the game once he stopped.

I must say I did miss it, but I was always involved in the club anyhow. I'd been secretary from 1975 till 1982. I was chairman of the club at that same time when I stopped playing... I was still involved and there was enough to keep doing with the club.

I missed it, because it had been part and parcel of my whole life running out onto a pitch... somewhere... but I never sat down and pined over it... nothing like that, no.

I never trained the team... I was involved underage and things like that, but never involved as a trainer with the seniors. I would have been a selector... on numerous occasions... while I was still playing I was sometimes a selector.... in 1975, '76, '82.... we had a mixture of players and non-players selecting the team down through the years.

And a few times since I've been a selector.

But never got involved as the man in complete charge of a team... I don't know why?

Maybe it's like taking a free?

Maybe I wouldn't be any good at it?